Time of Gratitude

Portrait of Gennady Aygi by Vladimir Yakovlev, 1973. Used with the permission of Ilya Umansky.

Time of Gratitude

GENNADY AYGI

translated from the Russian by Peter France

A NEW DIRECTIONS PAPERBOOK ORIGINAL

Manufactured in the United States of America
New Directions Books are printed on acid-free paper
First published as a New Directions Paperbook (NDP1394) in 2017
Design by Eileen Baumgartner

Library of Congress Cataloging-in-Publication Data
Names: Aïgi, Gennadiĭ, 1934–2006, author. | France, Peter, 1935– translator.
Title: Time of gratitude / Gennady Aygi ; translated from the Russian by Peter France.
Description: New York : New Directions Publishing Corporation, 2017. |
"New Directions paperbook original." | Collection of poems and essays.
Identifiers: LCCN 2017014036 | ISBN 9780811227193 (alk. paper)
Classification: LCC PG3478.I35 A2 2017 | DDC 891.71/44--dc23
LC record available at https://lccn.loc.gov/2017014036

10 9 8 7 6 5 4 3 2 1

New Directions Books are published for James Laughlin
by New Directions Publishing Corporation
80 Eighth Avenue, New York 10011
ndbooks.com

Contents

Translator's Preface

"Night is the best time for believing in the light." These words, attributed to Plato, are the epigraph to "Time of Gratitude," a cycle of poems composed in 1976–77 by the Russian and Chuvash poet Gennady Aygi. They mark the emergence from a particularly dark period in the poet's life following the politically inspired murder of his friend, the poet and translator Konstantin Bogatyrev – an emergence helped, as Aygi wrote more than once, by the example and inspiration of fellow writers from many countries. Aygi doesn't appear to have suffered greatly from the "anxiety of influence," and was very much a poet of gratitude, gratitude for the human and natural world, gratitude for the artistic creations of others. It seemed appropriate, therefore, to use this same title for a collection of tributes he wrote for some of the writers who meant the most to him, who enabled him to survive the spiritual and material hardships of a dark age in Russian life.

Gennady Nikolaevich Aygi (1934–2006) was the son of a village schoolteacher in Chuvashia, a non-Russian republic nearly 500 miles to the east of Moscow. His mother, a peasant woman, was the daughter of the last pagan priest of his village. After studying at the Literary Institute in Moscow and working for ten years at the Mayakovsky Museum, he lived and wrote in the literary "underground," remaining unpublished and unrecognized in Russia until the *perestroika* of the late 1980s. Thereafter, he became the Chuvash national poet, but it was as a Russian poet that he became known and published throughout the world – and eventually, after a long wait, in Russia. The English-speaking world was behind continental Europe in recognizing Aygi's importance, but several volumes of his poems have appeared in Britain and America over the years. In the introductions to two of them, *Selected Poems 1954–1994* (Angel Books, London, and Hydra Books, Evanston, IL, 1997) and *Child-and-Rose* (New Directions, New York, 2003), I give a general account of Aygi's work and career. *Child-and-Rose* also contains two important aphoristic essays on poetry, "Sleep-and-Poetry" and "Poetry-as-Silence," while a successor volume, *Field-Russia* (New Directions, New York, 2007) includes an important interview on poetry titled "Conversation at a Distance." These would provide a helpful background to the discussion that follows, where I focus on Aygi's involvement with the writers and painters to whom these tributes are addressed.

For Aygi, poetry was a calling, a commitment of the greatest seriousness. Even so, in an interview of 1985, he remarked: "In general I regard 'great prose' as the highest form of verbal art." He knew himself to be a poet, which was not the same as a "writer" – indeed, he described himself as a "non-writer." As a result, though he wrote many letters – a remarkable body of writing that should one day be collected – he was always reluctant to write publicly in prose: essays, memoirs, and the like. The texts gathered here were almost all written in response to pressing requests, for particular circumstances, anniversaries, deaths, special numbers of journals, new publications, etc. In a few cases, notably the text on Paul Celan, "For a Long Time: Into Whisperings and Rustlings," the prose is really a poem. And I have thought it worthwhile to intersperse the prose texts with actual poems, either because these are the only tributes he left to much-loved authors (Baudelaire, Norwid), or because the poems illustrate and illuminate the prose (as with those dedicated to Celan, Shalamov, and Char).

Reading Aygi's poems, one is struck by the frequency of dedications, quite often enigmatic, simply initials. They are addressed both to personal friends (all over the world) and to artists and writers, both living and dead. There is nothing unusual about this of course, but it is worth stressing that for Aygi poetry was essentially communication, the writing and reading of poetry creating scattered communities of people who could share a vision, a common search. This community crossed language barriers. Aygi himself worked closely with his translators, and he translated poetry from many languages into Chuvash.

It is worth stressing too that this village boy (and he did in fact remain a village boy in many ways until the end of his life, when he was buried in the snowy fields of Shaymurzino) became a citizen of the world republic of letters, a person of wide and deep culture. His poetry may lie outside the mainstream of Russian poetry as conventionally understood, but it creates its own tradition in which his native Chuvash culture (largely an oral culture until the end of the nineteenth century) flows together with European modernism (Nietzsche, and more lastingly, Kafka and Kierkegaard), the poetry of France, and the great Russian artistic movements of the early twentieth century. To these we can add (among others) many figures from earlier Russian poetry (one might mention Lermontov, Batyushkov, and Annensky), Russian prose writers of the twentieth century (notably Platonov and Shalamov), biblical and liturgical texts, religious thinkers – and in the English-language world (though none of them appear in this volume), the revered figure of

Dickens and poets such as Emily Dickinson and Gerard Manley Hopkins, insofar as they could be found through translation. At the same time, Aygi, who lived for a good part of his life in an underground world of writers, artists, and musicians, was much influenced by the other arts, notably the painters and musicians of the twentieth century – with Malevich as the central figure – but also, over a long period, the much beloved Schubert, who figures in many of his poems.

The first influences – the first debts – came from Vladimir Mayakovsky, whose impact on the young poet was great and long-lasting, even if he had to free himself from the "Mayakovskism" of which he speaks in his memoir of Boris Pasternak. The interview with the *Literary Gazette* published in this volume shows him resisting the temptation (strong in the post-Soviet era) to ditch the great bard of the Revolution.

In the 1960s, Aygi had worked in the Mayakovsky Museum in Moscow, where he organized several exhibitions of the artists of the early twentieth-century avant-garde (Malevich, Tatlin, Chagall, Guro, Larionov, Goncharova, and others) and acquired an exhaustive knowledge of the poetic and artistic culture of the period. As far as poetry is concerned, the two main figures apart from Mayakovsky were Velimir Khlebnikov and Aleksey Kruchonykh. As can be seen from "Leaves – Into a Festive Wind," Khlebnikov's legacy, like Mayakovsky's, was both positive and negative for Aygi; saluting his enormous achievement as a worker of the Word, he was bound to distance himself from what he increasingly saw as Khlebnikov's anti-human, "utopian" vision of revolutionary change, a vision which by the Brezhnev years had become inextricably involved with the crimes and horrors of the Soviet regime. Kruchonykh, whom he knew personally, seems exempt from such charges, and here Aygi is above all concerned to rehabilitate for Russian readers an experimental writer who was often written off as a joker, with his early intimations of sound poetry (*dyr bul shchil*) and concrete poetry. The piece on Kruchonykh is one of an unfinished series of articles introducing selections of poems by largely forgotten poets of the "Russian poetic avant-garde" – Guro, Bozhidar, Gnedov, Filonov, Mazurin. These, together with Georgy Obolduev (the subject of a much longer essay published under the pseudonym of A. N. Terezin in 1979) are more straightforward introductions rather than lyrical tributes, and also seemed too remote from the English-speaking reader to include here.

For Aygi, the central figure of this Russian avant-garde was undoubtedly Kazimir Malevich, not only for his actual paintings and three-dimensional creations, but for the ultimately religious vision of a non-objective art expressed in his writings on Suprematism. Unlike Mayakovsky and Khlebnikov, Malevich was in Aygi's view exempt from the political sins of Futurism; he always spoke of him with reverence, guarded preciously the few works of his that he possessed, and on one occasion took me to pay homage at the cube with a black square that marks the painter's burial place in western Moscow. He did not write at length in prose about Malevich (just the few paragraphs given here), but he dedicated several poems to the master, of which I've included the one that seems the most striking to me.

Almost equally important for Aygi in his early years as a poet was his contemporary the artist Vladimir Yakovlev, a tragic figure, and one of the leading figures in the Moscow artistic underground of the 1960s and 1970s. The artist and the poet inspired and helped one another, and Yakovlev left a number of portraits of Aygi, one of which appears as the frontispiece to the present volume. As well as some poetic notes devoted to Yakovlev's portraits, Aygi dedicated a number of poems to his friend, of which I've chosen two here.

Meanwhile, before his immersion in the underground, the young Chuvash poet had studied at the Gorky Literary Institute in Moscow. As well as contact with young contemporaries (such as Andrey Voznesensky), this brought him a vastly extended knowledge of Russian and world literature, but also the possibility of learning to read foreign poetry in the original. For Aygi, although Nietzsche was a enormously important liberating experience, the foreign poetry that mattered most belonged to France. He set about acquiring enough of the language to read Baudelaire – for him always the first poet of modernity – and eventually became intimately acquainted with the work of many other modern French poets. There are tributes in the present volume to two of these writers, Max Jacob and René Char, the first his "only moral support" during many difficult years in the 1960s, the second "not only a favorite poet, but a friend and teacher." Many other French poets were constant presences for him – Gérard de Nerval, Pierre-Jean Jouve in particular – even if he did not write separate tributes to them. And in 1968, he simultaneously paid homage to French poetry and enriched his own culture by publishing in Chuvash an *Anthology of French Poetry*, for which he was awarded a prize by the Académie Française.

It was while he was a student at the Literary Institute that Aygi got to know and love Boris Pasternak. The circumstances of their meeting are revealed in "Everyday Miracle," a text written more than thirty years after the conversations it describes. Pasternak was an enduringly important figure for the younger poet, and this in spite of the radical differences between their poetic ambitions.

When I first met Aygi in 1974, we walked through the woods and talked for hours about the writer known here as "the classic."

If Nietzsche had been the first overwhelming experience of European modernism, he was largely replaced in the 1960s by Kierkegaard and Kafka (both first read in French). There is no written tribute to the Danish philosopher, who was largely responsible for Aygi's return to Christianity. But Kafka, discovered for the first time in 1961, became the subject of several poems, and of the deeply felt piece translated here, "O Yes: Light of Kafka." In the same decade, Aygi first read another writer who was to have a key role in his thinking about the tragedies of the modern world, and of the Soviet Union in particular – Varlam Shalamov, the author of *Kolyma Tales*. This plainly written, immensely powerful evocation of life in the Gulag wasn't published in Russia for many years, but circulated in *samizdat*; first read in 1965, it became a talismanic work for young Aygi. It seems that the younger writer only met Shalamov once – on the rather difficult evening recorded in "An Evening with Shalamov," but his tragic themes echo through Aygi's verse for the next fifteen years. (The same is also true, though less directly, of Andrey Platonov's work, often alluded to by Aygi, though not the subject of a written tribute.)

As for poets, apart from the Chuvash, the Russians, and the French, the most significant figure was probably the nineteenth-century Polish writer Cyprian Kamil Norwid, represented here by the poem "Reading Norwid." In an interview in 1985, Aygi declared: "In the most difficult periods of my life, my thoughts turned frequently and intensively to Nietzsche and Baudelaire, and more recently to Norwid"; elsewhere, he wrote that two great Poles – Malevich and Norwid – had possessed the gift of "universal Language." For his knowledge of Polish writing

Aygi was much indebted to the dedicatee of this poem, his close friend and older contemporary at the Literary Institute, Wiktor Woroszylski, the author of the widely admired *Life of Mayakovsky*. It was Woroszylski who first translated Aygi and thus launched his international reputation. Having published his Chuvash anthology of French poetry, Aygi began work on a similar volume for Polish poetry; he recruited a team of translators, though he translated Norwid himself. Aygi also masterminded a Chuvash anthology of Hungarian poetry, and started to compile additional anthologies for Breton and Scottish poetry.

The literatures of two other countries figure significantly in the present collection of tributes: Sweden and Chuvashia. While Tomas Tranströmer was perhaps not such a talismanic figure as the writers cited above, Sweden was important for Aygi, not least because the Swedish cultural service abroad took an active interest in Chuvash culture – to this day, there is a thriving group of Chuvash poets, artists, and intellectuals who cultivate (with readings, music, drink) the memory of Sweden's national bard, Carl Michael Bellman. So Aygi was glad to write a preface to a selection of translations from Tranströmer, whom he loved and admired.

But of course Aygi's central concern was Chuvash culture, and I regret that it only figures in the present book in the form of an essay on Mikhail Sespel (as well as a section devoted to the poet Vasley Mitta in "Everyday Miracle"). Aygi's homage to his Chuvash predecessors and his native culture takes a different form, the *Anthology of Chuvash Poetry*, which he arranged to be translated into different languages (the English version appeared in 1991). In the introduction to this anthology, which ranges from ancient heathen prayers to poems of the 1980s, he gives an overview of the history, the culture, and the poetic tradition of his homeland, together with brief accounts of four of the most important poets: Konstantin Ivanov, Mikhail Sespel, Peder Khuzangay, and Vasley Mitta. A further act of homage to the poetry of the peoples of the Volga can also be found in his evocative little volume *Salute – to Singing: One Hundred Variations on Themes from Folk-Songs of the Volga Region* (Zephyr Press, Brookline, MA, 2002). The first sequence of variations ends with a heartfelt quatrain that could well be applied to the present volume:

> And where we stood
> may there remain
> the shining of our
> benediction.

—PETER FRANCE
Edinburgh, February 2017

I.

CHUVASHIA AND RUSSIA

A *Snowdrop* in the Storm

ON MIKHAIL SESPEL

Outside my window, the glimmering of the dim white November outskirts of the city is gradually becoming for me the place of a kind of forgetting... Where am I? – for a long time now, I seem to have been transported into some half-forgotten distant places... – and then to have begun wandering through a far-off, long-gone field amid snow-filled ravines – there were indeed such wanderings in real life, in just such a desolate twilight; it is hard in this dim and flickering darkness to draw a clear line separating dreams from visions, or from memories of something "real "

Somewhere, among those "eternally"-distant ravines which were once home to me, in a poor Chuvash village, in the November twilight of the year 1899, a boy-poet was born, one who would be forever a young-man-poet, dying at the age of twenty-two.... – he died more than sixty years ago, and *he* (not just an "image," but the *pain* within me) has not ceased troubling me, from my early years to the present day.

He chose as a pen-name the word "Sespel," which means "snowdrop" in Chuvash. The flaming tornado of the Revolution was raging through the land; its reflections were to the young Chuvash dreamer like the flashes and surges of his own inner world. At last, in the darkness of hopeless poverty, in the patriarchal stagnation of the life surrounding him, the long-awaited Thaw of his time had come – was he not the first flower piercing the snow? – timidly at first, and then ever more radiantly stretching out not just to the shining of the day, but – as he put it – to its fiery "transfigured face," stretching into the distance and depth of that "face" – he would always call it the "New Day," with capitals, and only in a poem written a few days before his death did the "burning concentration" of the New Day transform itself into the impenetrable "bottom of the Day."

He is one of the most tragic poets known to me, and this tragedy lies as much in the combination of circumstances in his life as in his own intimate nature.

He was not a "child of love." Half a century after her son's death, his mother would recall with unconcealed hostility the husband to whom she was married against her will. The memories of this illiterate woman, recorded from her talk, strike one with their almost Faulknerian details and images. On the night before her wedding, she dreamed of an ax gleaming on the threshold of a poor Chuvash house. This dream ax became real in the life of the family eleven years later: Sespel's mentally unbalanced father killed his own brother with an ax in a drunken brawl. He was condemned to forced labor in Siberia. As a boy, Sespel felt a *kindred spirit* in him – this half-literate peasant, devoid of any conception of "talent" and its links with "fame," was captivated by his son, who impressed him from childhood on with his lively imagination and grown-up thoughtfulness. "You'll be something no one has ever seen before," he used to tell the boy (and Sespel's unceasing longing for his father recalls Dickens's lifelong gratitude to his own weak-willed father for simply having realized his uniqueness and being "captivated" by him).

A year before the family tragedy, Sespel the herdsboy fell asleep on the wet ground when he was looking after the horses grazing at night. From then on, until the end of his life, he suffered from agonizing tuberculosis of the bone.

On his mother's side he was the grandson of a pagan priest – years later people still remembered this old man's remarkable mastery of the language of spells. And eventually Sespel's revolutionary poetry, his "spell-binding" energy, amazed readers with its wild, unbridled force, its unsurpassed vividness of language. During Sespel's adolescence there were periods when a crisis in his illness made it impossible for him to walk. His younger brother took him to school by sledge – a distance of several kilometers.

There was a rare kind of fire concealed in this sickly young man with his anthracite eyes; the deep-red flashes would soon begin to cut through his ominous poems, which showed not only a frenzied, perhaps even excessive, love for his native land, but also something "alien" to the language and the aesthetic ideas of his people. This genuinely Rimbaud-like fire came close to terrifying his compatriots.

And there was something Rimbaud-like too in his actions, which did not fit easily into the boundaries of familiar everyday life, the "quiet, sleepy" communal life that surrounded him. The young Sespel, like the young Rimbaud, left home (he didn't "run away"), abandoning his village schooling so as to take part in the continuing war against Germany; he got as far as the front lines, but grew disillusioned with his "patriotism" and returned home, becoming a supporter of the Bolsheviks.

It is significant that such passionate, reckless actions on Sespel's part, so unusual in his society, were never individualistic "escapades" – they weren't caused by any destructive tendencies, but by his deeply organic striving for the *ideal,* the urge to create new, ideally just, relations between people. Despite unimaginable material privations, he completed a course at a teachers' college in a small Russian-Tatar town (his heart aching at the knowledge that sometimes, in order to pay for her son's education, his mother had to sell her last bags of rye and she and his younger brothers go hungry). Given the provincial backwardness of the school, his education was extremely inadequate. His favorite reading was the banal, mediocre Nadson, but if young Sespel was a sentimental decadent in his letters of those years, once he started writing his own poetry, he immediately displayed a mature mastery of language.

Sespel became one of the first Chuvash Young Communists and was given work in the district criminal investigation committee. Sometimes, barely able to walk, he spent days and nights traveling through Chuvash and Tatar villages, torn between his unreserved support for the new order and his compassion for those who continued to live in the obscure poverty and degradation of "ordinary" life. In one instance, he had to investigate a major crime that involved a poor drunken peasant whose arrest left his large family without a breadwinner. Sespel, having obtained a harsh judgment against the criminal, kept sending money to the man's family from his meager salary (in the guise of "official aid"). Arriving in a Chuvash village on another case, he would go out in the evening after the day's investigations and help a needy family plow their piece of land. When speaking to the peasants, or at meetings, he was all thunder and lightning; but at friendly gatherings he was "neither seen nor heard." "I shared a little room with him over a long period," one of his friends remembered, "Mikhail had one striking ability – he moved about amazingly quietly. I was struck in general by his remarkable gentleness in everything he did."

In the spring of 1921, someone set fire to the building of the Chuvash Justice Division, and Sespel was arrested on the strength of a false denunciation. He was subsequently released (but expelled from the Communist Party), and went directly for treatment in the Crimea, his tuberculosis having gotten much worse. Once the treatment was over, the poet became a wanderer through an immense country, spending the last two years of his life in the Ukraine. A terrible famine had broken out in the regions bordering the Volga. "My country, my country is at death's door," he keeps repeating in his autobiographical writings, knowing that his voice will remain unheard. Working in the Ukraine as a famine relief instructor, he frequently came across groups of fugitives from the Volga region. "I see them at the station, starving people with terrible emaciated faces, in rags, fugitives from the Volga," he wrote in January 1922 to a Ukrainian friend. "In the recent hard frosts they were dying in droves in one place or another, sick, freezing people; their bodies were loaded by the hundreds onto sledges and driven away, open to the elements... In the market place, where masses of goods are being sold and there are rolls and loaves of bread, lard, everything you need, these fugitives from the Volga lie barefooted, covered in sores, and dressed in rags – they beg for bread without saying a word...." He wrote this at a time when he was crippled by tuberculosis of the bone and barely able to limp along. He knew he was doomed: "My body is disintegrating like a corpse, there's no stopping it," he wrote in his diary as early as 1920.

During his lifetime, Sespel had fewer than ten poems published in Chuvashia. Strange poems, in places "nearly Chuvash" with their incredibly daring imagery; they seem almost "wildly alien" when set among the old-style half-folkloric syllabic verses of the period. And now, in the far-off Ukraine, poetry became for Sespel the hidden inward space (an almost anatomical place) where his inner spasms found a "suffocating" expression in convulsive lines of verse.

There is certainly something of Mayakovsky in him. But strangely, he showed no particular interest in him. Was it that he was wary of a kind of ego-nucleus in Mayakovsky's tragic stance, a kind of self-infatuation of the Russian poet in his own tragic fate? When Sespel, on the other hand, at the height of spiritual tension, moved deliberately and resolutely toward his own destruction, his "metaphors" (but are they metaphors? they're not Mayakovsky's famous "heart on fire," elaborately constructed on formalist linguistic principles), his "similes," and images are torn out of the pain of his very being, like clots of blood ("All bloody – What is this in my hand? / I break it, turn it to dust, to meat, / Tearing the veins. It is my heart, / Mine, Mikhail Sespel's bloody heart"). How opposed to folklore is this poet whose origins lie deep within the people! But as the years pass and I think of him more and more, I seem also to hear, behind the "scraps of meat" of his metaphors, something of the secret "murmurings" of the people, something "not spoken to anyone" that emerges like a muttering-and-whispering ("who can hear it then?") in the depths of that "silent speaking" that was half-chanted, half-muttered by the people – and that "secret chasm," as I see it now, seems to glimmer elusively yet steadfastly behind the light-and-darkness of Sespel's poetry.

I have remarked elsewhere how Sespel, true to the modesty and discretion of the people, never allowed himself to *aestheticize* the tragic. He might well have flung this tragic element in the face of contemporary poetry in images equaling those of the Surrealists, but this would have been a narcissistic "literary" act for him; in Sespel's work it is the people who "cry out," not the poet. Did he even realize that tragedy had found in him an exceptional *mouth* (more than a voice)? He had no time to realize it, he had to *finish crying out*, incarnated in the "crucified body of the people." Or rather, this incarnation was there from the *very beginning*, but now everything was growing confused: where he had once "cried out" – was it him? – everything went silent, as if all meaning had been taken away, and this silence grew into the emptiness of a sudden, indefinite Abandonment; it became a kind of single body, and then – this was now the only source of breath still continuing – the ghost of a cry: "Eli! Eli! Lama Sabachthani!..."

Perhaps he could feel death entering into him, as the young Trakl no doubt felt it – but isn't the Austrian poet spellbound by the allure of death, like some blue, blue beauty?

Sespel's move toward death wasn't a "settling of scores" with life. Was he "needed" or "not needed" (not for destruction, but for creation)? That remained the essential *problem* for Sespel, right up to the hour of his death. "I am no longer needed, I must *remove* myself, this will happen very soon," he said clearly, quietly, and calmly to his last friend, a Ukrainian peasant poet. "Think again, Mikhail." "I'll think, and I'll tell you what I decide, I promise." For once in his life, Sespel did not keep his promise. One day soon afterward, he failed to return to the house where he and his friend were living. He had taken his own life in an avenue of lime trees near the village of Starogorodka in the Chernigov region.

The officials who came to investigate the cause of death took away most of the poet's papers, which never resurfaced. This was the second great loss of his manuscripts, the first being when all his papers were seized upon his arrest in Cheboksary in 1921. His poetic legacy is now about thirty poems – they are the unequaled masterpieces of Chuvash poetry.

1983

Henceforth

(THE LAST DROPS OF BLOOD)
By Mikhail Sespel
Translated from the Chuvash via the Russian of Gennady Aygi

Henceforth, turned into stones, in heaps,
The warm word, frozen, has stuck in the throat,
From the forest top day's light has fled,
And death lies over the world henceforth.

Barefoot on to the Hill of Torment
They have led my country, led her by the hand.
The bloody sweat of the walls of Cheboksary
Is held in my shattered heart henceforth.

All bloody – What is this in my hand?
I break it, turn it to dust, to meat,
Tearing the veins. It is my heart,
Mine, Mikhail Sespel's bloody heart.

Like a dog that has had its hide ripped off,
I shall beg a crust in a stranger's yard,
Some drizzly day I shall drop down dead,
Hungrily howling for Cheboksary.

Henceforth from my innards, dried up with hunger,
Will come only the groan of the cold graveyard,
My soul will be filled with a massive millstone
Henceforth, henceforth, henceforth...

1921

Everyday Miracle

MEETINGS WITH BORIS PASTERNAK (1956–58)

1

I am writing of a Poet who possessed an *Apollonian* beauty at the age of seventy and of an ecstatic twenty-two-year-old... myself – "and I cannot draw a line between us": not between myself now and myself then, nor between them both and the *divinity* of the Poet whom the young man adored.

The different ages of my life merge together here, and I cannot help it, let the naive appear in all its naiveté and contradict a certain belated detachment from my earlier passion.

At the time I was a student at the Moscow Literary Institute. The student residences were in Peredelkino, and I shared a room there with my friend Rim Akhmedov, the Russian-Bashkir writer.

Akhmedov recalls (in the Ufa newspaper *Leninets*, February 10, 1990): "Aygi's relation to Pasternak's poetry underwent a transformation, just as mine did. At first, in 1953–54, he fiercely resisted my attempts to knock into his head what already seemed to me basic, elementary truths. He went after me furiously, made fun of me. Some time later he began to reflect and to confess reluctantly: yes, maybe there's something there. Then, having reached a certain stage of invisible mutation in his way of thinking, he suddenly saw the light and exclaimed: 'But he's a genius!' And living through Pasternak's poetry became as much a daily necessity for him as ritual prayers for a believer."

And now, one May night in 1956, I was walking back home – from my first meeting with *my divinity*. A few hours spent with

Boris Leonidovich on the veranda of his dacha felt like some enormous, whirling fusion of Shakespeare's *Tempest* and *Midsummer Night's Dream.*

It was past midnight when I arrived back in the room I shared with Rim. My friend, who had been waiting impatiently for me, exclaimed, "What's the matter, have you been crying on your way home? You're all wet!"

"I don't know whether I'm wet from my tears," I replied, "or from his kisses. He kept kissing me so much...."

This was how I entered the immense world not only of Pasternak the Poet, but of the older Friend, the Teacher, the unparalleled Interlocutor.

2

He was wholly under the spell of the novel he had just completed. He seemed surrounded by the power of an endlessly expanding Freedom, in which there rose up an unending inspiration, shifting and soaring from one level to another, all-embracing and irresistible.

And indeed the theme of *freedom*, in connection with the novel, dominated our conversations. Boris Leonidovich often wove variations on it. He would proclaim openly, unhesitatingly, "We can see now the beginning of an unheard-of spiritual freedom – not only is it embracing Russia, but it will appear in different forms all over Europe."

I reacted reticently to this. Later, after his death, I used to think that he had deluded himself, attributing to an imagined future the impulsive power of his own freedom. I defined the culture of our times as a *post-Auschwitz culture*, which was represented for me, in spite of chronology, by Mandelstam and the OBERIU writers; Pasternak, as I saw it, did not belong to this culture – not because of some kind of "anachronism" on his part, but because of what I saw as his "conciliatory-harmonious" nature.

It was only in October/November of last year, 1989, when I was in Italy and Scotland and learning with amazement like all those around me of the unheard-of changes taking place in Eastern Europe, that I began to remember Boris Leonidovich's words about "the beginning of an unheard-of freedom." I am convinced that it was indeed *this freedom, a freedom of this kind* that Boris Pasternak perceived in the 1950s.

In my presence he never complained of the "narrowly-topical" interpretation of his novel – by certain people around him; perhaps such a reaction was perceptible only in his repeated assertion that "they have a very true understanding of the novel in Europe, a broad understanding."

Once he asked me, "You're a reader, you're interested in everything, do you know Camus?" I replied that I had heard of him but had not read any of his books. "I haven't read him either," Boris Leonidovich went on, "but I feel that he is very close to me, a *spiritual brother*. It seems to me that he has understood the essence of the novel better than anyone. I get astonishing letters from him. He has called my novel 'the Passion of twentieth-century man' – after these words, no further definitions are needed."

He spoke excitedly of a letter from a monk (a Dominican I think), who had written to him, breaking a long-standing vow of silence, "Just imagine: a silent monk – and me. He calls me his 'brother in spirit' – just what I feel toward Camus. It turns out that even he can find help in my novel. And how *contemporary* his letter is – its style, its ideas! – You couldn't imagine anything like that here."

We talked about the *poetics of prose*. Once, he began to speak about Dostoevsky: "What is the art of depiction in prose? Balzac, for example, writes fifteen or twenty pages describing a street, a town, a house, then he goes on to his characters, and we have already forgotten the street and the town and lost sight of them. But what an art of depiction there is in Dostoevsky! He never specifically describes a town, a square, the streets, but his hero moves through it all, he suffers and acts, and we see vividly the surroundings where all this is happening."

"What is prose?" he said another time. "It is a place where *everything* must exist *simultaneously* – like Breughel, you know."

In our conversations about the novel and indeed in all our conversations one theme kept recurring, that of the *presence of the miracle* in ordinary, everyday life – "in everything" (I shall have more to say about this shortly). I once said in passing to Boris Leonidovich that it was precisely the "disjunctions" whether of plot or other elements that created the "atmosphere of the magical" in his novel, and he listened to me in silent agreement.

At our second meeting he asked me a question with some embarrassment, slowly and hesitatingly: "Tell me... You are a man... of the people... forgive me for talking like this!... Tell me, does my novel seem to you not to be *ours*?"

I was staggered – it was as if all the depth of suffering of my incredible interlocutor was revealed to me. "Boris Leonidovich, what are you saying! It's ours, it's *ours absolutely*!" In the ardor of my reply I was almost choking. Pasternak threw his arms around me.

I wasn't aware that a lot of people kept annoying him with their nit-picking deciphering of details in the novel. Once this happened with me too. "Boris Leonidovich, you really love Antipov, don't you?" He gave me a rather puzzled look. "Or rather, you *like* him," I corrected myself. "It's as if you admired him. As you admired Mayakovsky. And generally, there seems to be something of the moral beauty and straightforwardness of Mayakovsky in him. And there's his name: Anti-pov...."

"It never entered my mind," he replied. "But 'beauty and straightforwardness'... Yes – I admired *that kind of beauty* in Mayakovsky and in Meyerhold too, even though we had opposite beliefs. I loved them, I admired them...."

There was a lot of happiness related to his novel and my conversations about it with the author himself. The difficult times (as I experienced them) came very suddenly – like a single immense, dark avalanche. In the early spring of 1958, Boris Leonidovich was waiting for me as usual on his veranda. He didn't stand up to greet me. He was sitting with his arms clasped around his bent head with its splendid silver-gray hair. Hearing me arrive, he dropped his arms and his face seemed... charred.

"Boris Leonidovich, has something else happened?" I exclaimed.

"*The clouds have gathered around my head again.* They are accusing me of not accepting the Russian Revolution, of slandering it."

Everything in this exclamation hit me at once, and I was struck by such a deeply concentrated, almost "childishly natural," rephrasing of Pushkin. In my confusion, I said very naively from the point of view of "form" (as for the substance, I still think the same), "But the Revolution is like a force of nature. After all, when the sun rises, there's no question of accepting it or not accepting it."

"Exactly!" he started choking with painful exclamations. When he had calmed down, he said slowly and distinctly, "The question is not that I did not accept the Russian Revolution; I accepted it as Mayakovsky did. I simply believed, and still believe, that *it remained incomplete.*"

In our own day I listened with amazement to a statement by the present leader of the USSR about the *second revolution* – since this was said by Boris Pasternak, *in substance, and with exactly the same meaning*, all of thirty years ago (even sooner indeed, in the historical essence of *Doctor Zhivago*).

3

I arrived in Moscow from Chuvashia in the autumn of 1953. In the "Chuvash backwoods" it was hard to get hold of books. I had read and reread what there was so often that while still a boy I started going around the nearby villages looking for bookworms like me. Alas, I didn't find anything new through them either.

I came to the capital knowing only Mayakovsky of the Russian poets of the twentieth century. I adored him; for a long time I imitated him, distorting my own way of writing, my own "lyric voice," over many years.

Boris Leonidovich sensed very clearly this "presence of Mayakovsky" in me. And I don't think a single one of our meetings passed by without touching on the author of "A Cloud in Trousers."

"Mayakovsky was like that, but I..." – this was a frequent refrain in our tempestuous conversations. There were whole "Mayakovsky monologues": "You had to *see* him, see him in the flesh! He was the *physical* incarnation of genius in human form!" – and then followed a whole flood of explosive definitions that I cannot resurrect now.

One time I commented on what Boris Leonidovich had said about the period in Mayakovsky's writing that he "didn't understand," or "didn't accept." "If he hadn't had a 'committed' period," I said, "if he had gone *straight ahead*, charging down the line of his early tragic poems, the next 'poem-act' would have been his suicide."

"Yes, I see 'At the Top of my Voice' as a delayed suicide," he replied.

I believed, and still believe, that at that time there were two equally powerful poetic poles: Mayakovsky and Pasternak. I believe that Boris Leonidovich was aware throughout his life of the constant force of the *Mayakovsky pole* and reacted to it; the quarrel with Mayakovsky, the assertion of his own values as the opposite pole (the "antipode"), were present, as I see it, in the final elaboration of the design of *Doctor Zhivago*.

From the very beginning, my conversations with him were so much concerned with general questions about creativity and existence, developing into a kind of "inspired poetry," that the names of other poets were mentioned only in passing – almost by chance.

"Khlebnikov was a poet of genius, but he didn't write for people," he remarked one day. I could easily have raised objections. But I didn't, knowing what the expression "to write for people" implied for him, namely not to invent any kind of "project," but to be capable of saying the word that is *most essential*, like bread, for one's *people-brothers*. Generally, it is very great people who permit themselves to say "evidently impermissible things." I love the old Tolstoy with his "impermissible things" – I am sure that he was a "secret example" for Boris Leonidovich. It seems to me that Pasternak's famous "heresy of unheard-of simplicity" grew closer over the years to Tolstoy's "heretical heresy."

Rilke often permeated our conversation, like air or light. Moreso because at the time of our first meeting, I had already read the *Notebooks of Malte Laurids Brigge* in the two-volume Russian edition of 1913. (It is amazing how few people were familiar with this edition in educated Moscow circles – you could look for it in vain even in some of the best private libraries.)

Any mention of other poets, as I said, was insignificant. Boris Leonidovich nodded his agreement when I spoke of the "constructed" quality of the poetry of Aseev and Tikhonov ("Yes, of course, 'constructed' is right; but if I don't say anything about them, they'll be offended" – we were talking about his autobiographical "People and Positions.")

At one point he mentioned the "brilliance" of the early Zabolotsky ("He was once very gifted"), but clearly wasn't aware of his subsequent fate: "And he might have become a great poet."

He treated the enormous correspondence that followed the publication of *Doctor Zhivago* as a kind of creative work, even if it "took up a lot of time." "The other day I received a letter from the Rabindranath Tagore Museum. You must know how popular he was in Russia, just before the Revolution; I sensed a kind of spiritual confusion in all that – Tagore never appealed to me. Even so, I found something to say about him in my reply to the Museum."

In 1957, I was translating Aleksandr Tvardovsky's *Vasily Tiorkin* into Chuvash. Boris Leonidovich asked how my work was progressing. I found the work burdensome, having been forced to do it to earn some money, and I tried to brush off the question. "You're wrong," he said. "Overall, it's the best thing written about the last war. And his Russian is beautiful."

Then he added, "Do you think I translated Shakespeare and Goethe out of love? I love them in any case. But I, too, was forced to take on the work in order to survive, to *keep going*."

In the autumn of 1956 I introduced Pasternak to Nazim Hikmet, who considered the Russian writer to be "the greatest contemporary poet." Hikmet said to me, "I should love to see him, of course, especially as he lives so close. But he must be exhausted by these constant pilgrimages."

"Not at all, Nazim," I objected. "Believe me, he's very lonely. Just go and see him – 'just like that.'" Nazim was reluctant: "I don't know, I don't know. He'll say, 'Here's another 'peace campaigner.'"

A few days passed. One morning at the Literary Institute, Irina Emelianova (Olga Ivinskaya's daughter) rushed up to me: "Gena, Nazim came to see the classic yesterday – they sat on the veranda and kept embracing one another till morning!" (Irina and I used to refer to Pasternak as "the classic.")

In October 1958, I met Nazim by chance in the lobby of the Moskva Hotel. "It's shameful, shameful, utterly shameful!" he kept repeating in a depressed tone when I started to talk about the "Nobel scandal."

In the autumn of 1956 there was a rumor at the Literary Institute that Pasternak had agreed to meet the students there (such meetings with "older brothers in literature" took place regularly). The rumor was confirmed. "What do you think of this?" Boris Leonidovich asked me. I expressed doubt: maybe the students "in the mass" would not understand him. So was it worth it?... Though personally I would be very glad to see him there.

"Even so, I've decided to agree to a meeting – for just one reason: *I want to talk about Pavel Vasiliev*, what a gifted poet he was; I've never ceased to be amazed at the power of his poetry."

The times were changing rapidly. There was another rapid shift of ideological direction at the Institute, and Boris Leonidovich's meeting with the students did not take place.

Recently I read that Pasternak shocked Anna Akhmatova by his "deep indifference to all the poets who were his contemporaries." I have no intention of trying to rebut this well-known opinion – such a "judgment" doesn't belong to my generation. Let me repeat that in my meetings with Boris Leonidovich I felt in the atmosphere a kind of "freedom of the spirit" (something more than the merely "personal," it seemed). This spirit was constantly concerned with the *very great* and very important in literature that remained a lasting example for him ("Incidentally, Goethe," I can hear his voice – "and as for Proust..." – I can hear it, but I cannot remember the exact words). I did not ask him about the great poets among his contemporaries, I simply abandoned myself to the power of his Freedom – this mattered more than "literary problems." And this Freedom allowed him to discover where he could soar in the expansive flight of its magnificence.

One day Boris Leonidovich was giving me his impressions of Van Cliburn playing the piano (I remained skeptical about his colossal triumph): "The genius comes along and abolishes all the laws that existed before his coming, laying down his own laws."

If we may dwell on this "personality factor," I can perhaps say that I, too, interested him not as the representative of a generation, but as an individual whom he had met and become interested in. (He gave a "primally-broad" significance to the individual. In such a context anyone who revealed themselves to him was a complete world, in which the Pasternakian Freedom just mentioned spread its wings.)

Not long before my meeting with Boris Pasternak, another major event occurred which even today still continues to define my "spiritual orientation." In 1955, the outstanding Chuvash poet Vasley Mitta returned home. He had been arrested in 1937 at the age of twenty-nine and spent seventeen years in Stalin's prisons and camps. I had known about him from childhood; he had been a friend of my father, who was a village schoolteacher, a verse writer, and one of the first translators of Pushkin into Chuvash. It was really only for two years that Mitta enjoyed a state of free, creative work (at the height of his mature powers) – in the summer of 1957, he died in his native village during the great popular festival of "Agadui." The festival came to a halt and the poet's funeral was attended by thousands of people.

For understandable reasons, Vasley Mitta didn't write a great deal, but he left dozens of poems which have become the most precious masterpieces of Chuvash literature. In all of Mitta's acts of self-expression (poetry, letters, conversation, actions), there was always something "Socratic" – a modest and laconic reminder (that was *poetic* in its *beauty*) of very ancient and valuable elements in Chuvash ethics and aesthetics.

I recently read the posthumously published notes of my acquaintance the Russian priest Sergey Zheludkov about Andrey Sakharov. "I observed in Sakharov traits of *personal sanctity*," he wrote. I can say that such "traits of personal sanctity" were observable also in the Chuvash poet Vasley Mitta (and, indeed, he is regarded as a national *saint* in his homeland).

Being under the spell of "brother Vasley" (as we called him in Chuvashia), I spoke excitedly to Pasternak about him. Boris Leonidovich asked detailed questions about the Chuvash poet; then, while declaring that he had not "earned the right to say anything special to anyone," he asked me to pass on to Mitta his rapturous words about "the fortitude of all the martyrs" of the hell of Stalin's camps – words of sympathy and hope.

"Brother Vasley" listened to this oral "message" from Pasternak, then said quietly and unhurriedly, "Please tell Boris

Leonidovich that when those of us who were involved with literature met in the prisons and the camps, we always said to one another that *Pasternak is free, he is faithful to Conscience and Truth, and consequently truth still lives in the Word.* His very *existence* helped us to preserve our belief in life."

At that time I often traveled between Moscow and Cheboksary, and thus acted as an intermediary for a "conversation at a distance" between two great poets. I was in Irkutsk when I learned of Mitta's death from a very brief obituary in the *Literary Gazette*. Soon afterward, I returned to Moscow and almost immediately went out to Peredelkino. Boris Leonidovich was expecting me at the appointed hour and came to greet me. His first words were: "How could it happen? How was it possible? I keep saying to myself: how improbable it is – *could they have done something to him*? He wasn't even fifty."

And now, less than a month ago, one of my friends sent me a copy of a Vasley Mitta letter, found in the archives of the Chuvash KGB. Mitta had sent the letter to a Chuvash writer from the Writers' House in Maleevka, just outside Moscow; it is dated January 30, 1935. I was astounded to find in it the following lines: "Yesterday was a very important and significant day for me. Pasternak came to visit us here. He's an amazing man. Pasternak, like his poetry, is extremely hard to understand; it's very hard to grasp his personality. But at the same time, you feel in his presence an immense, irresistible force, the presence of an exceptional spirit, like an unusually stormy, indefinable *music*. What power, what an immense generosity of soul! – you can't express it in words, you can only *feel it*." How surprising that in our conversations about Boris Leonidovich, Mitta never mentioned this red-letter day of January 29, 1935!

During our last meeting, in the spring of 1959, Boris Leonidovich asked me if I knew the poetry of Andrey Voznesensky. I replied that I had read only one poem by him, "Goya," and that it had "left its mark on me." "Yes, he's very gifted. I should like it if you two were friends. I am sure that you will become friends," he said. Having spent three decades out of contact with "literary life," I met Andrey Voznesensky only in December 1988, in Grenoble. Now, of course, Voznesensky and I remember these words as our common "inheritance" from Pasternak.

I particularly want to record that Boris Leonidovich possessed a remarkable feeling for the spiritual-intellectual "baggage" of the person he conversed with.

During the three years of our meetings (sometimes weekly, sometimes twice monthly), I had always wanted to discuss Nietzsche (in those years I was utterly impregnated with Nietzsche's *aesthetics*, and in *this* respect I considered him my "spiritual father"). But I felt instinctively that I should not raise the subject – a discussion of the German philosopher might cause discord between us.

And then, at one of our meetings, Boris Leonidovich started to talk about Nietzsche of his own accord. It was a tumultuous conversation, full of enthusiasm on both sides. "In my young days everyone was a Nietzschean, Gorky just as much as Mayakovsky (I won't even speak about the *lengths* to which Leonid Andreev and others took their devotion). I wasn't one of them – they were carried away by Nietzsche's amoralism. For me Nietzsche was above all an *aesthete*, an *artist*. If some beings from another planet landed on earth and said, 'Name *one of you* who most completely embodies the *artist*, the *man of art*,' I would have replied, 'Nietzsche, only Nietzsche!'"

It was growing dark, we were sitting on the veranda, our knees almost touching. In his excitement, Boris Leonidovich began hitting my knees with the palms of his hands... and I started doing the same.

Afterward I called in on Olga Ivinskaya. "How did you find him?" she asked. In that difficult year, she liked me to drop in and see her after my meetings with Boris Leonidovich "so as to know how things are with him, to keep in touch."

"Today we were thumping each other," I joked awkwardly. "About Nietzsche." And I told her about our conversation.

"Never!" she exclaimed. "He's always criticizing him. Just a week ago he was saying negative things about him, while writing about Kierkegaard."

4

He didn't really want me to talk about his poetry. He would shrug off my references to the poems of *When the Weather Clears*: "There's a lot that is hasty and fragmentary in it, and what's worse, people are always getting hold of the first versions and circulating them in manuscript, while I am trying to bring some unity to it all."

Once we nearly quarrelled. On my way to see him, I walked for a long time under the unusually shaggy tops of some lime trees, and I kept hearing a line from Pasternak's "Second Ballad": "With shovels as when leaves are falling...."

I entered with this rhythm in my brain, and immediately blurted out something about the "Ballad." "Don't you know I can't stand people talking about my early verse!" he roared at me. And in the same angry tone of voice, he started off on how it was all "redundant and mannered, precious, unnatural," etc., etc.

At this point I started *shouting* too (probably because I felt instinctively that there was no other way out of the situation): "Yes, I've heard *plenty* about how you *ruin* your early poems, Boris Leonidovich! You're wrong! They're *classics* now, and they don't belong to you. There are thousands of readers who know various poems of yours by heart; they won't accept your current revisions. You can't take what you have created away from me; it lives in me, quite independently of you. And what's more," I went on more peaceably, "let me tell you why I raised this subject that annoys you so much...."

And I told him briefly how I had been walking beneath the "seething rags" of the lime trees and had felt myself "included" by everything that exists, the world, the Universe – "everything, absolutely everything."

"What? You felt that? You *understood* it?" Boris Leonidovich's *roaring* took on a different tone. "How splendid, really! You understood it...." The conversation continued in its usual peaceful manner. We never returned to the subject of the "unnecessary complexity" of his early poetry.

In the 1970s, when I was living a more solitary life in various Russian villages, in the midst of Russian nature, I became convinced that the incredible "simplicity" was for me the "incomprehensibly-simple perfection of Creation" (the most mysterious thing of all that "exists"), necessarily and antinomically yoked together with the agonizing problem of its relation to "verbal simplicity" – in my "own special understanding." I won't go into that now (let me simply say that I clearly have some "trouble with the world of things") – concerning this question, my "individuality" causes me to diverge somewhat from Pasternak, but at the same time I marvel at his incredible daring, his courage and his sense of responsibility toward the

Word that is essential for humanity, the *reborn-religious* Word – seeming as it does to carry the fresh seal of immediate Grace.

Even so, Pasternak's "heresy of simplicity" in his later years – in relation to the *means of expressiveness* – began to assume an excessively "penitential" character (as if he had "left something undone"). Thus one day he asked my opinion of the poet B., whose "simplicity" was really a kind of folkloric stylization.

"Yes, I already know your special feelings toward him," I answered. "That's why I've read something of his. It's a strange mixture of particular artistic elements and verbosity."

"Yes, there's a lot of water in it," he replied in a rather dejected voice.

5

I have already mentioned that the *second subject* that ran through our conversations, and all our meetings (enclosing them in a broad, "pulsating," luminous embrace) was what might be called the "hereness," the "everyday" presence of the *miracle*, the miracle of the Creator and Creation – although none of our conversations were "specifically" religious. (My religious feelings at that time were highly abstract, in the "Hegelian" mode. I was obscurely and tentatively moving toward a "Pascalian" position, but any decisive involvement with Russian theological philosophy was hampered, above all, by my wary attitude to the "Sophist" Vladimir Soloviev.)

Boris Leonidovich raised the subject at our second meeting. "The miracle is quite simple. It's all round us, constantly. When you read a text, you are communicating not with letters but with the spirit of the author – you are communicating with *the man himself*! A miracle – and you, sitting here opposite me, that's a miracle too."

Perhaps it's time for me to say that, speaking for myself, I regard it as simply impossible to reproduce the unique qualities of Pasternak's speech. In essence, it wasn't even "speech," but a *storm of inspiration*, the ardent coming into being of a thought, associations, explosions of *direct feeling* (almost like "interjections"), that seemed to strike directly to the soul, as if from one body into another. In writing his words down as direct speech, I am giving merely a schematic account of what he said.

Only once did I attempt to "fix" the storm of Pasternak's speech (and this was several years later). On May 26, 1965, a *strange evening* took place in the town of Zhukovsky outside Moscow devoted to the "Ninth International Festival of Young People and Students in Algiers." The first two items on the program were devoted to the problems of Algeria and the UAR, followed by:

III. B. L. Pasternak. Poems. The following will speak about Pasternak: N. V. Bannikov, editor of "Literary Russia"; Gennady Aygi, poet.

The Pasternak part of the evening was a flop. The organizers were on edge due to the presence of a group of "plain-clothes art historians" in the hall. Bannikov, who had been at work that day, "fell ill" and didn't turn up. One could sense that the audience knew little about Pasternak the poet, and I spoke so chaotically that I should have disappeared into the earth. Before the meeting, I had written out a few pages of my speech. Let me quote a surviving fragment:

"In order to give you some idea of Boris Pasternak's personality, I have decided to describe one meeting with the poet. What happened on that occasion needs no commentary; it is enough simply to transcribe it, since it is in itself like a perfectly shaped work of art.

"In the summer of 1958, I was on my way to Peredelkino, hurrying to the Literary Institute where I was a student. I had difficulty in taking cognizance of the day: I was very late for work and what's more I was in the company of a student whom I had often seen among the nationalistic gang at the Institute. At a junction just beyond the Peredelkino cemetery I wanted to turn right. Then I saw Boris Leonidovich. He was dressed in a white raincoat, and heading straight for us. I won't try to describe him: I can hardly have noticed anything except that *he* was there in front of me, as indefinable as a natural phenomenon.

"He embarked on a tumultuous monologue: 'What a shame – I can see you're in a hurry – what a morning! – you've no time – what a lot I wanted to say to you! – you understand me! – you must understand! – you haven't much time! – but you'll see: the main thing – the most important thing – here, this morning – the trees – you – that sky – all at once: this world – all at once – nature – the sky – those pine trees! all this at the same time and understood together – yes, that's what I wanted to say to you! – I want you to understand it, to accept it – straight away, all together! – let it all be with you! – you've understood me, haven't you? – you must understand it!'"

I should add that before I could notice anything, Boris Leonidovich disappeared behind the pine trees. My astonished student companion stood there goggle-eyed: "*Is that really Pasternak?*"

At the end of the same year I went out for a walk with my wife; it was nearly midnight. On the Peredelkino crossroads, just by the electrical transformer box so well-known to many of us, we came face to face with Boris Leonidovich. This happened, incidentally, in the middle of a *very Pasternakian* snowstorm. It was into this elemental turbulence that Pasternak's true "snowstorm monologue" flowed: "That's wonderful! You are here at last! And people think that the meaning of existence, its essence, what is most important in it, is somewhere *there*, 'in other worlds!' No, everything is *here*, now, in the present moment! The eternal, the abiding essence is *here*! And we are beautiful *here*, and the secret, the miracle, our eternity are all *here*! You do understand, don't you?"

This *snowstorm monologue*, of which I have given such a feeble representation, stayed with me for a long time, like some weightily-living world; it became a sort of *content* in my mind. Later I wrote a poem titled "Here" – my poetic credo – for which I am totally indebted to Pasternak.

Boris Leonidovich said to my wife, "I know your husband got better a few weeks ago. I was waiting for him to come and see me. As always, it was like waiting for a blessed meeting. And anyhow, why does he come to see me less often these days?"

"It's because he's not keen on two students who are constantly visiting you, Boris Leonidovich," answered my wife. "He sees them as calculating in some way."

I felt uncomfortable and couldn't stop myself bursting out, "No, you can't...."

"No, she's right, I understand, I understand," he answered warmly, then, turning to my wife, said in a voice which was now quiet and gentle, "You're right. But you know, you can't measure friendship with a thermometer."

6

A lot has been said and written about Pasternak's "egoism," his "self-centeredness." Once he himself raised the subject with me. It was as if he was *complaining.* "They all accuse me of egoism. Those who are close to me have a lot to put up with, I understand that. But tell me, *is it really egoism* to take in all nature, all suffering humanity, all the incredible beauty of the world, to absorb it endlessly into yourself so as to give it all away – expansively, generously, unreservedly – to share it not with anyone in particular but with anyone, everyone!"

My generation grew up without fathers. The few pseudo-fathers who remained in the literary world fought with people like me as if they were equals. In my youth, I only met with a genuinely paternal attitude toward me from two Chuvash poets (one of them being Vasley Mitta, whom I have just mentioned) and from Boris Pasternak.

I was unhappily in love, unhappily married (I blame only myself for this – my foolish impetuosity and the chaos of my life). Just before my short-lived marriage (I was in my last year at the Institute and still living in Peredelkino), Irina Emelianovna came to see me and gave me a message from Boris Leonidovich inviting me to visit him with my future bride: "I would like to give him a father's blessing, since he grew up without a father."

I had a sense of the shakiness of what was happening and *didn't dare* go and see Boris Leonidovich. He felt that there was something amiss in my "personal" life (at this time there were also signs of the imminent punitive measures against me at the Institute). One time he said to me, "When things are going badly, try to find some *domestic* task. When you're in that kind of state, *writing* can be impossible. Even *translation* can be difficult, heaven knows. Find something old to copy out, retype something, busy yourself with little technical corrections. In such circumstances, women have the instinctive wisdom to get on with the washing, the ironing, or the sewing."

(I must add that many years later, when I was in extremely difficult situations, I tried deliberately to find domestic activities, so-called "women's" activities almost – and did so remembering Boris Leonidovich's advice).

In March 1958, I was expelled from the Literary Institute and from the "ranks of the Young Communists" for having "written a hostile book of poems, undermining the foundations of the method of Socialist Realism." Boris Leonidovich took this as a blow against himself. We met straight after the event – and mutely agreed not to discuss it. I simply said, "This is a logical development of destiny; I've been following this path for a long time now, and in a way I feel calm about it." He nodded silently.

But some time later there was a rumor in Peredelkino that one of the students at the Institute had committed suicide. Boris Leonidovich headed for the dormitory, and asked the first group of students he met about me. (This rather surprised me, but then I came to understand his particular worry – he could see that I was taking the breakup with my wife badly, and this came straight after the business at the Institute.)

Incidentally, the student who committed suicide was the same one who had met Boris Leonidovich by the cemetery and asked in amazement, "Is that really Pasternak?" He left a note in which he said there was no other way out of the "surroundings" that were tormenting him.

I need to say now that the "throwing overboard" of the fathers from the "steamship of modernity" seems to me a natural law of literature and to a certain extent of the general "game" of life. As it happens, I began to throw my divinity – Boris Leonidovich – "overboard" even while he was still alive. For instance, in the presence of a certain highly cultivated Jewish family, I suddenly said that I couldn't accept the theory of "Jewish assimilation" in *Doctor Zhivago*: "It's easy for him to talk about such things." My hostess called me a "traitor." A few years later, I was criticized by the same family for my moderate attitude to this same "theory" of Pasternak's. (Soon afterward, this family, who remained friendly toward me, left Russia.)

I also began to express "anti-Pasternakian" attitudes (concerning some aspect of his poetics) in conversations with my friend Rim Akhmedov. After listening to what I had to say, Rim exploded: "But do you know that only a week ago he *came here* at night to ask about your health? And did you ask yourself how we managed to pay for not only your medicine but even the oranges we have been feeding you?"

Let me quote from Akhmedov's memoirs: "One day my friend Aygi fell seriously ill. He tossed about in a fever all night, delirious. I was pretty scared, and the following morning I didn't go to work but hurried to the Peredelkino medical center to call a doctor. The doctor determined it was a double inflammation of the lungs. He wrote out a prescription and said that a nurse would come around to do the injections. He prescribed mustard poultices and recommended a good diet: fruit, milk, broth. We only had a few rouble notes in our pockets, and on the table only a loaf of cheap bread and a couple of onions – our lunch and supper. It was enough for me, but what could I give him, the invalid? How could I buy medicine? I'd have to borrow from somebody yet again until my grant arrived. I was heading gloomily for the station to catch the suburban train when someone called me from behind. I turned around and saw Pasternak. He must have seen from my face that something bad had happened. He asked me why I wasn't at work. I told him Gena was ill. Boris Leonidovich was distressed and began asking for details. It was the first time I had seen him so upset. As we talked he mechanically walked a few paces with me, then suddenly stopped, took me by the shoulder and muttered with some embarrassment, 'Listen, I'm afraid I have no money with me just now. But come with me, we'll find something.'

"I followed him obediently to his house. We went up to the study I knew so well. Boris Leonidovich took several twenty-rouble notes out of the desk drawer, hesitated a little, then took out some more and handed them to me, saying, 'Go to the chemist's first, then buy something to eat at the shop, something as tasty as possible.' I thanked him with great emotion, stupidly repeating that as soon as my grant came I would repay him. He frowned and muttered: 'Wait till you win the Stalin Prize, then you can repay me.'

"In the street I counted the money: two hundred and fifty roubles, half my grant. I could easily repay it all at once, particularly since I was earning a little in a factory, where I also ran a literary circle. That same evening I stuffed my friend with medicines, applied mustard poultices, gave him tea to drink, and fed him with smoked salmon sandwiches that I had bought in the pathetic little station buffet. He cheered up.

"The next day brought a surprise that we hadn't at all expected. There was a gentle knock at the door, and Boris Leonidovich walked in. He had come to visit the invalid. I had just taken the poultices off Aygi, and he had fallen asleep, exhausted. With a quick glance, the visitor looked around our cramped little room, with barely space for two beds and a small desk between them. On the table was a cheap gramophone in a plastic case. On the walls by the bedheads were portraits of Voloshin, Nietzsche, Mandelstam, Akhmatova, Pasternak, and Tsvetaeva, sketched in charcoal on Whatman paper, and copies of Masereel woodcuts and of Van Gogh's drawings "Melancholy" and "On the Threshold of Eternity." All of this was the work of my unskilled hand. A slight smile touched the corners of Boris Leonidovich's lips.

"He sat down on a chair next to the sleeping invalid and placed the palm of his hand on his hot forehead. He asked me what medicine I was giving him. I grumbled that Gena was fussing, that he couldn't keep the poultices on for more than an hour – children put up with it but he wouldn't. Boris Leonidovich was horrified and explained that they mustn't be kept on for more than a quarter of an hour. He lifted up the blanket, looked at the scalded red chest, and shook his head. He gave me some more advice, and before he left, he placed some apples, two lemons, a tin of concentrated cocoa, and another fifty roubles on the desk. Some time later, when I tried to return the money to him, he reproached me in such an offended tone that I blushed, crumpled up the money into the pocket of my ski pants, and didn't know where to hide myself for shame."

I felt a pure joy from my friendship and conversations with Boris Leonidovich. I never wanted anything from them. (For instance, I didn't ask him for manuscripts or copies of new poems – the thought never entered my head.)

In the summer of 1958, when I found myself without a Moscow residence permit or any money to live on, I went off to Irkutsk, to the family of Professor M. M. Lavrov (the grandson of V. M. Lavrov, the editor of the Slavophile journal *Russkaya*

Mysl'). I was going off into the unknown, for an unknown period of time. Before leaving, I said goodbye to Boris Leonidovich. He insisted that I should write to him: "I'll reply without fail." I used to compose in my head enormous letters to him, but I felt that they might turn out "terribly literary" and unnatural, and I never wrote to him. (In these "oral letters" I wrestled helplessly with a swarm of thoughts and feelings, as if I was struggling with the whole "Universe.")

After Boris Leonidovich's death, during the very painful (but still not "unendurable") quarter of a century that followed, I often wondered how Pasternak had managed to survive that terrible half-century of Soviet life. I remembered many things, including various "everyday details" (which I won't mention in this recollection, keeping them "for myself"). I thought of his powers of endurance as a kind of mystery. It seems to me that the explanation of his ability to endure and conquer is this: As I saw it, Boris Leonidovich possessed a *genius for enchantment* – for being enchanted by all kinds of things and at any moment: a falling leaf, a child he met on a walk (even today the "ordinary folk" of Peredelkino still remember him: "Pasternak was the only one of the writers who greeted us"), a dark rain shower, a stranger he talked to, or as he would have said: "everything, everything" – life, the Universe, his own poetic Creation of the World.

7

At our very first meeting we discussed my poetry. Or more precisely, we spoke about a Chuvash narrative poem – roughly six typewritten pages long and titled "Beginning" – in a line-for-line translation which I was stubbornly "hammering out" for two years beginning in 1954. Boris Leonidovich gave his opinion in one sentence: "Half of it I like very much; half I don't like at all."

I didn't even ask him to explain. I could clearly see which "half" he didn't like – everything with traces of "Mayakovskism" in the "anatomization" and "physiologization" of the images.

In the autumn of that year into the next I read him half a dozen lyrics and a short narrative poem devoted to the Czech poet Jiří Wolker ("Is he really such an important poet?" he asked). I remember particularly well my first reading. Boris Leonidovich listened completely absorbed, his face growing darker and darker as if he plunged into some element – I have never known anyone who listens to poetry as attentively as he did, whoever was reading. He asked me to repeat one passage in the poem about Wolker ("and little red lamps burn as quietly and intently, as if little Pimens were sitting in them, quietly and intently writing that the chronicle continues").

He remarked that the scientific terms I introduced into the poem "are effective in emphasizing the inner contours of a single image – and your poem is like one single image – you are right to use these terms, but not as often as you do."

As if he was summing up his overall impression, he said, "As a rule you immediately discover the 'zone' where the *nucleus* of the image is to be found and then you start reinforcing its wider impact. But you haven't yet reached the point were you throw out the good in the name of the better."

I later wrote that "this one sentence became an enduring poetic lesson for me."

I also read to Boris Leonidovich my Chuvash translation of his "Winter Night." He hugged me and said, "But the shoes fall to the floor earlier in your poem than in mine." And indeed, I had transposed the stanza with the "little shoes" in my translation.

When I read him one of my free verse poems in Chuvash, he asked me, "Does it really sound like that?" "Yes," I answered, realizing to my amazement that I had indeed given to the voiced consonants of the Chuvash a sharpness similar to the Russian sounds.

On several occasions I had the impression that he was avoiding one particular topic – that my "line-for-line" versions of Chuvash texts were beginning to seem almost like translations. So once, as if justifying myself in some respect, I said to him that as I saw it, "the thing in poetry is to achieve beauty, and it doesn't matter which language you do this in."

"I agree," he answered thoughtfully. "But I have the feeling that you have already entered the flesh of the Russian language, and done so rather boldly. What's more, it seems that only writing in Russian will allow you to articulate fully everything that is happening within you, in the way of an emerging poetry, as we talk. You are probably hesitating over the choice. If you asked me whether I consider if you are capable of going over to Russian, I should answer: Yes, I do. For you are already in a Russian-language world."

Hikmet, when he talked to me on the same theme, had no hesitations: "You need a large instrument. You need an orchestra. There is no question you must go over to Russian – it will correspond to what you possess in yourself. But remember: *They will never forgive you for this move* – that you, the son of a small nation, will exist within a great literature. I tell you this from my own experience. Our experiences are related – I too have had to pay a price for migrating into the European context."

I was making the painful move into Russian in 1960, during the months when Boris Leonidovich was already fatally ill. One of my first Russian-language poems was "Winter Marked by

God." This title contains a secret "quotation" from Pasternak; I knew that with those close to him he referred to me with the words: "He is marked out." The large volume of my poems in Russian that came out in Paris in 1982 bears the same title. (This was my way of preserving the "legacy" of Boris Leonidovich – secretly, for myself alone.)

I also always remembered the following words as a "legacy" of this sort: "Your oneness with nature is close to my heart. But I would like to say one thing: that a time will come when you will have to make a deliberate effort to preserve this *gift* as a kind of duty you owe to your own work."

On our penultimate meeting, at the beginning of 1959, Boris Leonidovich said, "Russia is a happy place for the artist. The bond between man and nature has not yet been broken here."

8

In the autumn of 1959 I went home to Chuvashia, to be with my dying mother. In our house I lived "under official surveillance, as a hostile element," according to a statement at a session of the local regional executive committee.

There were frequent letters from Moscow, from Irina Emilianova. Then suddenly they stopped. And one night I had a visit – a secret visit – from two young men from the next village (both had been expelled from some Siberian institute for "ideological reasons"): "We have heard a lot about you. They talk about your relations with Boris Pasternak. So we decided to tell you that foreign 'voices' are broadcasting that he is seriously ill."

Some time later I received a telegram. I was pierced between the eyes by the words that leaped off the paper: "*Classic deceased.*"

My mother, a peasant woman who had had little formal education, possessed a strongly developed mind and was for me a true *spiritual friend*. I used to tell her about Pasternak – she understood his significance in my life. "You absolutely must go to his funeral," she said. "Please go. Trust me, I won't die before you get back."

Night fell. I went hurrying over the fields to the distant regional center, from which I could continue on to the railway station. The moon was shining brightly. And suddenly I decided to read the telegram again. It said: "Funeral Tuesday."

Boris Pasternak had been buried three days previously.

My mother died exactly two weeks after Boris Leonidovich.

Thus – with this terrible double blow – my youth came to an end.

JUNE 7–13, 1990

Requiem Before Winter

IN MEMORY OF BORIS PASTERNAK

I shall follow and remain like a silent choir
in the space of god all the preordained day
alongside the shifts of the clear winter day
as alongside soot

but time is of itself self-created
hurled into the world snow whirls
round the monastery gates
and the inevitable passers-by
seem now support from without

but the level of the century is already fixed
and the level of fame demands
that the face be turned toward quietness
and not a book but an atlas of passions
is preserved in quiet on the desk

but like soot the year will touch the houses
in the old century where books seem torn up
and any of the pages will demand
lines of cutting and folding inward
across my sleeves
with the cold and the window nearby and outside
the snowdrifts the gates the houses

1962

Leaves – Into a Festive Wind

FOR THE CENTENARY OF VELIMIR KHLEBNIKOV

The human being first participates in language through *childish babble*. Is this true of poetry too?

Yes – in the writing of Velimir Khlebnikov.

In his poem "The Sea," a poem that is magnificent in a near-Pushkinian way ("classical" as Pushkin is classical), we suddenly hear the words "to the boat wa-wa, sea's a nasty man, sea has done bo-bo."

Remembering this "done bo-bo" (meaning "hurt"), I reread the whole poem. It contains so many "childish things" that it seems clearly to have been composed in accordance with an "infantile method" (one or two more examples: "Waves leap tsa-tsa"; "Sea, sea, da-da-da!"; "Sea weeps, sea blubs").

There are lots of interjections (hot, as if fresh from the as yet untrained lips of a child) scattered through Khlebnikov's poems.

In the most serious situation he will suddenly express himself, syntactically speaking, in a childishly "incorrect" way: "Into the 93rd foot regiment I perished as children perish." (This example was once used by Roman Jakobson in a different context.) The outline of his images sometimes recalls the directness of children's drawings: "And the bridge scratched with the nail of a Footsoldier running off to one side" – that is *strange,* genuinely strange, both grandiose and infantile, all in a single brushstroke.

A discussion of the "language of different ages" (or "age language") in Khlebnikov could go on ad infinitum, throughout his poetry. Take the long poem "The Crane," which astounds one with its wealth of images of universal uproar (in them we hear the roar of a kind of gigantic Unity of the city and the sky above it). These images are openly clumsy; we feel in them something of the "mechanism" of the excessively logical, angular, intrusive arguments of Dostoevsky's "raw youth" in the novel of that name, in a word, a "raw-youth clumsiness" – and this is one of Khlebnikov's poetic devices.

In defining the work of a writer it is useful to have recourse to the concept of his or her *linguistic conduct*. In most writers, a variety of linguistic devices are contained within a single, characteristic language. But in Khlebnikov one can see also *many kinds of linguistic conduct*. In his poem "Thickets," the stern war cry of the warrior chief slips easily into the sound of a minuet, the archaic language of the wise bard ("Stag, oh stag, wherefore does he weightily / Bear the word of love on his horns?") is interrupted by a childishly-helpless exclamation ("No safety, stag, no escape") – rather like the childish cry of the Holy Fool in Pushkin's *Boris Godunov*: "But I've got a little kopeck."

*

the bonfire as an exclamation of Khlebnikov

*

In the age of Khlebnikov, Russian poetry ceased being *élite* poetry (I'm not thinking here of its accessibility to "all and sundry," but of the "program" of the great poets). More than this, the hierarchical *ranking* of the poetic word within individual creative systems was abandoned; this feeling of "emancipation" of the word did not, however, eliminate aural sensitivity, which remained impeccable in the new "democratic quality" (as opposed to the complete loss of "ear" in the servile literature of the late 1930s).

There is no contradiction between this and the fact that Khlebnikov distinguished in poetry between the "language of the stars," the "language of the gods," "senseless language," and so forth. (We have a rough draft in which he lists the levels of language he uses – a total of twenty different "languages." It's true that this classification displays a fair degree of spontaneous poetic *illusionism*.)

Attributing a *cosmic* meaning to language, Khlebnikov was indeed obliged, as far as possible, to "liberate" the word from its "earthbound communicative nature"; he achieved this "liberation" not by denying the word its status as *logos*, but by making it radiate an unfamiliar, hallucinating light. To serve his general purpose, he had recourse to "everything" (as was the case in Nikolay Fyodorov's "philosophy of the common task").

This "everything" will eventually be studied by the linguists. But for the present, in writing these "festive leaves," I have jotted down a rapid list of some of the "discoveries" of the Russian avant-garde concerning the "periodic table of the elements" of poetry – a kind of Mendeleev-Khlebnikov table.

What did Khlebnikov do earlier than other poets? "Visual poetry" began with Apollinaire's *Caligrammes* and Vasily Kamensky's "ferroconcrete poems," both in 1914, but there is a draft of Khlebnikov's manifesto "The Letter as Such" dating from 1913, which already argues for "lettrism" and anticipates "visual poetry" – and in 1915 he wrote a "poem of numbers," now lost. "Object poetry" began in 1913 with Kruchonykh's "trans-sense pook," with one of the author's trouser buttons sewn onto the first copy (okay, let's give this "Duchampian" button a mention); in 1915 Kamensky exhibited two "poem-pictures"; "emotional" or "secondary" *trans-sense* (*zaum*) made its first appearance around 1911 in a poem by Elena Guro, but the first genuinely trans-sense texts were created, independently of one another, by Aleksey Kruchonykh and the Ego-Futurist Vasilisk Gnedov. Gnedov, whose name is still only known to a few literary specialists, was a unique character. He was the first representative of Russian "anti-art": his "Poem of the End" a blank page the poet "conducted" in public performances. I was lucky enough to see Gnedov in 1965 at the Mayakovsky Museum in Moscow, at a celebration of the eightieth anniversary of Khlebnikov's birth. During his speech, Gnedov referred several times to Mayakovsky by the familiar name "Volodya"; there were sniggers in the audience, whereupon this stocky, strongly built Ukrainian with his "identikit" peasant face and seventeen years in the labor camps behind him, *barked out*: "Don't you laugh at me! I put even Mayakovsky in the shade when I appeared alongside him!" (Let me note in passing that Khlebnikov quotes Gnedov in one of his poems.)

As we can see, various names figure in this listing of poetic "discoveries" and "innovations." But the original impulse behind them was Velimir Khlebnikov – his catalyzing personality, the omnipresent "Khlebnikov spirit," a legend in his own lifetime.

But that is not all. The most important of all these "beginnings" was Khlebnikov's *word-creation*.

How the poet sometimes desires, not to *speak* with the definitive *logos*-word, but to *ring out*! – to resound with a kind of absolute beauty of the beautiful! – as in music. Khlebnikov's "word-creation" was the first breakthrough toward this "absolute beauty," which continues to demand from the poet almost superhuman efforts; the "absolute" remains unattainable, but it is precisely this ever more evident unattainability that gives poetry its incandescent quality.

We should also note here that Khlebnikov's first composition, a prose piece entitled "The Temptation of a Sinner," which laid the foundation for root word-creation, was published in October 1908, four months before Marinetti's first literary manifesto.

*

with blue of the velimir soul
they cut – the baby-pure "woads"
with an innocent sound
both the voice of a child and a wise
peasant's gaze – and the roads
in the one Field-Russia
in one coming together in one diverge:
somewhere long ago in velimir features!
I too am in some ways a little face
as it were – made from almost mussorgskian pain!
and they cut – as they heal – the sadness through silent fields
in the roads of the bending face – at this minute
with latent blueness – the "woads"

*

The searching, the hopes, and the achievements of the century, its illusions and its spiritual defeats, were expressed, as I see it, in the personality and the work of Velimir Khlebnikov not by *truth* in the philosophical or theological sense, but by *rightness* in the revelation of the essence of poetry: his immense labor in liberating this essence meant that language had to function like a "universe" – from the splitting of the "atoms" of the word to the intellectual "ordering" of words-stars – as the poet himself would have put it.

If Khlebnikov's work had been simply coterminous with the circle of the Russian "poetic avant-garde," it would be no more than a series of Duchamp-style happenings, whose meaning would be confined to a self-consuming singularity with no further development – or with at best a pseudo-development.

The Tatar raids of the "avant-garde" on unknown "poetic territories," even in a single year (1913), were enough to last a century. One "landmark" after another was laid down, one poetic "discovery" followed another, each one more daringly projected into some kind of distance, some "future." These "landmarks" remained on the great map of Poetics, but the territory itself remained "unexploited," unfortified – it simply remained empty, and in many ways is still empty today.

Now it is we who have to work on these "lands," and our task is clearly a thankless one. We have to inhabit – stubbornly, patiently, "unsensationally" – the territories over which the troops of the avant-garde marched victoriously with no old-fashioned, hard-working, spiritual concern for their "earthly" state. To inhabit them, to fill them with a spiritual content, one cannot live by "landmarks" alone, one must live and work the earth, whether it brings forth fruit in our time or not.

That's how things would be (and for us, who are responsible for our own time, that is indeed how things *are* in many respects), if it were not for Kazimir Malevich, and if we had not received the enormously rich inheritance of Khlebnikov – objectively-concrete in its historicity and unprecedentedly polyphonic in its "transformation" of so many domains and nooks and crannies of the "language of linguists" into new poetic resources (including the resurrection of "pan-slavic archaism" and the alchemical transmutation of the "cells" of words) – all these elements used with great scope and, at the same time, on many levels (I am thinking above all of the great vaults of his epic poems).

Here, of course, one should mention Mayakovsky. But that is another story (the complex interplay of his poetics with the Cubo-Futurist avant-garde needs to be studied afresh – the essence being that his tragic poetry, as we now see it, seems to lean more and more toward the central tradition of Russian classical lyricism of a moral-confessional type).

*

> wounded by Khlebnikov's "bullets of the sun"
> I shudder – as if glancing around
> out of corners – made by self-shocks
> of the landslips of sleep! lit up
> by whiteness – broken by many
> soullikenesses from depths of oblivion
> clear-eyed – without faces

*

But at present, in discussing Khlebnikov more than anyone else, we need to be concerned with things other than poetry.

This discussion is a matter of necessity today, and to be frank, I don't greatly care if certain points in it seem out of proportion to so important a phenomenon as Khlebnikov.

"Velimir was a poet of genius, but that wasn't enough for him – he wanted to be a prophet as well," Aleksey Kruchonykh once said to me.

And that was indeed the case. But prophecies have one special characteristic: on Earth, as far as we know, they are always negative, or premonitory. "Positive prophecies" are very agreeable... until we realize how closely connected they are with the human *cult of self* (which is, if you think about it, no more agreeable than the cult of individual personality).

It seems that mankind has been living under the sign of social utopias only for the last five hundred years or so. One cannot, therefore, claim convincingly that utopianism is mankind's eternal ailment, part of our once-and-for-all essence.

Many ideas of Khlebnikov's day, and in particular the "futurological, socially prophetic" ones, have receded into the past. Even those of his predictions that have been fulfilled only bear witness, as I see it, to the beginning of the end of all utopias (though we shouldn't be too hasty with such categorical statements – we human beings are very stubborn children of God).

"We want to speak familiarly to the stars" – we read that now as a piece of "poetic eccentricity." The stars continue to be as they were for Tyutchev, not interested in speaking to us familiarly or otherwise; perhaps all they want is to be left in peace.

In his day, Andrey Platonov had an attack of this new (universal) disease: utopia (Khlebnikov did not have time to follow the course of this "disease" to the bitter end).

When the weight of the "conditions of human existence" broke the *axis* of Platonov's personality, broke it like a bone, he became a man "like all other men" – "the insulted and the injured." In a philosophical sense, he felt existential sympathy with the very "simple" people, those who "simply" suffer. (Someone can have an aching kidney and, you must understand, it may be more important than any "cosmic" problem, and similarly you can have an aching "soul" – genuinely aching, like your liver.)

In one respect, Khlebnikov's "cosmic" illusions and "cosmic" sufferings left their mark on Platonov – something entirely new in Russian writing entered his relation with words; his words became impregnated with an indefinable "universality," a new "enlarged" pain of existence.

*

> and the stars
> there
> are pure (and will be eternal
> if Time
> is abolished) pure
> innumerable and lonely – and these
> are the eyes of Velimir
> the Last
> and the First

*

"And meanwhile" (an expression from a brilliant fragment of Khlebnikov's prose) – and meanwhile there has been only one human discovery on Earth. An American scientist, the son of a German novelist, has refuted the expression "the bestial cruelty of people," saying "the human cruelty of people."

There is a striking scrap of paper with drawings by Khlebnikov – "houses of the future." And indeed it foresees the future in detail. These houses have already been built in places. And they have received a new name: "clever houses."

The House-Flower. The "cleverness" in this house is the hearing. It busies itself listening in on me borrowing a few dollars – "to keep going." The convenience and splendor of these "houses of the future" are linked in the most direct, "regular" way to the impoverishment of what we call "souls."

I apologize for raising such trivial everyday issues in talking about a major phenomenon. But such trivia are an essential part of the present-day criterion of humanity, and this criterion – the suffering and endurance of human beings – is caught between enormous, formless dreams and the despair of reality.

The whole content of the classic work of the French scholar Alexis Carrel, *L'Homme, cet inconnu* (Man, This Unknown Being), can be summed up as follows: throughout human history, we have been more concerned with studying the world around us than ourselves.

We exist in a truly "new age," opposed (in its experience and intellectual orientation) to that of Khlebnikov.

"Not to plan, but to endure" is how I would express this difference. To endure – to understand the true measure of humanity, which is not slight, but is simply *other...* – how can we define it? – perhaps human beings, always mindful of their mortality and weakness, have to learn to create a world that seemingly belongs to them in the sense that our universe-world also suffers pain and death, and that *respect* for this universal suffering is given to mankind as an expression of a common suffering. In such a *common fate,* even on the other side of mortality, humanity remains responsible in the face of what exists "non-anthropologically," a responsibility devoid of the desire to twist it according to our own will.

Let me say a few words about this "twisting" or "not twisting." Can we be concerned today with respecting the "stars," the "world," like our own pain, like a broken "branch" (as I am)?

Here is one more possible future utopia: a sort of "post-ecological faith" (a dimly glimpsed "sacred fear and trembling" in the face of that same "branch" – just touch it, and the "irremediable" will become yet more "irremediable" and perhaps "final").

Without believing that, I want nevertheless to say once more how I see humanity's place in the world, our way of living in it. One could put it like this: "I suffer, as the world suffers" – and there is a link between these two sufferings, with no distinction between the small and the immense, since suffering is not measured as something more or less "great" or "small"; this compassionate and irrevocable bond is indeed the essence of humanity; in other words, that "by which we live and stand firm" – it seems we have no guarantee of an "end," even if, perhaps, we desire it.

*

"I have built timber huts" so you yourself said
o poetic
walls of logs of metaphors shiningly-solid
with a spacious-natural clang
like the air – at a time of labor!
pure "workman's" wood
more than ninety percent
with no rubble of required "poeticisms" –
just as peasant households
contain no luxury

I have read Khlebnikov's poem "Three Sisters" dozens of times. The descriptions of the "sisters" are such that reality seems to be continually intersected by "clear-sighted" lines that reveal something lying beyond nature, beyond the intellectual "substance" of people, beyond everything "visible and perceptible."

"Yet I am god's" – one day the poet let fall this "plaintive" sentence. So what is this god? – you will not find an answer to this question anywhere in Khlebnikov.

Though possessing definite mystical gifts, he was strongly inclined to the type of religiosity that established itself precisely during his lifetime. A certain "abstract faith" that survived through the centuries took the form in his time of a "religion of scientists" – something newer than ordinary "deism." The existence of a power transcending reason (an "impersonal" power, moreover) was now demonstrated not simply by "enlightened reason," but by "scientific reason." What a new kind of freedom and clarity, you might say, a *rationalistic religion* – in a highly irrational world!

I don't want to go into details (in general, our age seems to me to be one of *crude affirmations*). Let me simply say that within this global humanity marching "beneath the banner of Lobachevsky" through "the expanses of Tsiolkovsky" (the visionary rocket scientist), I can yet again see mankind not triumphant, but "simply suffering." (The religious element in Khlebnikov that is bound up with his scientific enthusiasm I also see as "poetic magnificence.")

The "simple man" not only "has the right" to believe in a personal manifestation of what he senses as a "higher" power; in his respect for the existing world – the *creation* – he is individually responsible to this "high-personal" power.

This is not an abstraction or an anachronism, nor a "return

to the past." The truth of what we might call the words and commandments of Bethlehem continues to be proved today, in a negative way, by the very world we live in, with all its entropically *degenerescent* aspects, infected as it is by the virus of self-destruction.

There is really no dispute about this; there is simply a lack of understanding – one person does not believe in something in which others believe (or vice versa, those who believe in one thing do not believe in another).

Khlebnikov did not put temptation in the way of the humble; he himself was tempted (and was there ever such a time of temptation? – humanity itself split apart in the "incarnation of the idea in the word," and there is no human *reality* other than this "incarnation"). And today, I do not believe that it is the poet's fault if some people continue to be tempted by those "good intentions" of his which have outlived their time, and which have been outlived by his poetry.

Khlebnikov's poetry has one quality that is probably the most important thing that exists in him. The sound of his poetry sometimes seems almost "babyishly" pure. I have already spoken of its "raw youth." Yes, he is often awkward, like Don Quixote. But a Don Quixote who knows himself, with a kind of deep, mysterious wisdom. Sometimes there is the flash of a searching gaze: "Ah, that's how you react, but just wait and see what comes next." After the fearful cascade of words in his stern rebuke to his contemporaries ("For ten years the Russians stoned me"), we again hear the almost childish voice: "But I am god's."

It's always a case of "Wait and see."

And whatever I may have said here, his image always emerges pure from it all, truly innocent and pure – let me stress that without reservation.

I hope that this "Don Quixote" discussion will not irritate some of Khlebnikov's admirers. The ways of spiritual victory are mysterious – sometimes they appear in an unexpected place. Khlebnikov's poetic exploits are of a kind that can only be achieved by throwing yourself headfirst into the craziest struggles with the word.

"Wait and see" – but Khlebnikov gave enough to last us for many years. Even his "Don-Quixotism," in the end, is swallowed up in the all-encompassing roar of his epic creations; there is in this roar something cinematographic too, but something not yet achieved by any filmmaker. And you can hear in it a kind of pre-Schönbergian *Moses and Aaron*, an all-inclusiveness which in its unity seems just the beginning of a music of infinite grandeur – whose name is the *poetry* of Khlebnikov as the future will reveal it.

*

and it gleams the blue-eyed soul
from the net of spectral "laws of time"
and the face is ever clearer: nearer and more transparent
of one who loved ears of corn like a child

*

These leaves of paper are swept up by the whirlwind of festivity; everything whirls – from Earth to Heaven – and perhaps the Universe too begins to swirl. Everything is mixed up: the subtle predictions of his mind – Kazimir Malevich said that he was a man of *um* (mind) rather of *zaum* (trans-sense) – the light from crumbling bones, the distant shouts of the preachers of reason and unreason, the blinding light of word roots, the "lightning-sisters" of his Pythian metaphors, the banners and expanses of the "world beyond" – everything flows together in the rainbow colors and lights of the infinite world of Poetry.

*

wounded by Khlebnikov's "bullets of the sun"
I finish speaking – and I shudder
through suburbs and ruined centers
of seeing and unseeing sleep
of sleep-disintegrating-me
and the operation is to awaken
on the 29th at nine
of a Moscow-suburban morning

*

MOSCOW
SEPTEMBER 23–29, 1985

Yes, Kruchonykh Himself, or The Least Known of the Most Famous

In the history of Russian poetry there has possibly been no greater injustice than that which has been done, and is still being done, to Aleksey Kruchonykh.

Our literary scholarship has never attempted to seek out what is essential in his work. Kruchonykh was needed as a "scapegoat": for half a century the "sins of the Futurists," Vladimir Mayakovsky and Velimir Khlebnikov, have been deflected onto him.

Krucha, Krykh, Kruchik, Kruchen, Kruch. "Forgot to hang myself, flying to America!" *Zudesnik, zudar, zudivets,* and his poems in *Zudutnye zudesa.* "Masters of precision, having sealed our ears with wax so as not to hear the sirens' serenades, we shout like alarm clocks that delicate hearing cannot endure: *rrrrrjjjtzzzziiiii!...*"

Mayakovsky deafened his hearers; Kruchonykh woke them up, got on their nerves, "drove [everyone] mad" (but in life, among friends, he was the most peacable of men).

His sharpness, his irrepressibility, his deliberately planned stunts, the way he popped up everywhere, his unfailing witticisms – all this allowed him to be seen as a "wonderful eccentric" (as Mikhail Svetlov put it). This was indeed the "positive reaction" to Kruchonykh of many of his friends and acquaintances ("Kruch" was strikingly sociable) – it's a way of rendering poets harmless, as Velimir Khlebnikov has been treated up to the present day.

"For thirty years I've been trying to clean out people's brains in relation to Kruchonykh," Nikolay Khardzhiev said to me when we first met in 1961. Maybe he managed to clean out half a dozen.

It was easy to be condescending to a poet who was rejected by society. I saw him drawing his pension; if I remember rightly, it was thirty-one roubles. Kruchonykh hadn't been published since 1930 (symbolically, this dividing line was the year of Mayakovsky's death). I have never met a more joyful poet. In all circumstances, he was artistic and aristocratic. These qualities harmonized miraculously with his Russian peasant appearance – the lines of his face suggested a kind of rustic enlightenment and even, for all his anticlericalism, something distantly Orthodox.

"I have three whales supporting me," he used to repeat with pride in the last years of his life, "they won't let me fall."

He meant Malevich, Khlebnikov, and Mayakovsky.

Yes, he was Malevich's favorite poet. "Only Kruchonykh has remained in me like a rock, unswerving in his love for the New God, and he remains so still," the great Suprematist wrote in a 1916 letter to M. Matyushin. And Mayakovsky subsequently trumpeted this slogan-like phrase about Kruchonykh: "A genuine poet, a cultivator of the word!"

Out of habit (as Kruchonykh himself did), we are still citing authorities for our literary rehabilitation of the poet of trans-sense (*zaum*). But Kruchonykh has no need of this on the world stage. For the last twenty years there has been a "Kruchonykh boom" in European literary scholarship, with endless articles about the poet and some fundamental academic research.

A remarkable literary theorist and linguistician, he was responsible, with Khlebnikov, for stirring up the linguistic thinking of his time. The year 1913 saw the appearance of

"The Word as Such," a joint declaration by the two poets; here the art of poetry is seen as the liberation of the hidden possibilities of the "self-valuing" word (its acoustic nature, etymology, and morphological structure), anticipating the theories of OPOYAZ, the Russian Formalist school.

The jointly authored writings on literature and linguistics by Khlebnikov and Kruchonykh are becoming steadily better known. But there are also theories elaborated by Kruchonykh alone, above all his ideas about the *faktura* (texture) of the word (he wrote of a "difficult, heavy *faktura*," a "rapid, light *faktura*," of the "splinteriness," or the "extremely rugged surface," of verbal material). He was also much concerned with *sdvigology* (the theory of the *sdvig*, or shift in perspective). In his "Declaration of Transrational Language" of 1921, he gave the following basis (among others) for poetical *zaum*: "Randomness (the alogical, the accidental, the poetic impulse, the mechanical combination of words: slips of the tongue, misprints, lapses; this includes, in part, acoustic and conceptual shifts, national accent...)" Elsewhere he notes: "Incidentally, Freud writes about shifts, slips of the tongue, misprints, and the like in his *Psychopathology of Everyday Life* and *The Interpretation of Dreams*."

With his keen awareness of sound, Kruchonykh laid bare all kinds of "shift" within traditionally "sweet-sounding" poetry. (He infuriated many people by discovering "lions hearing and seeing" in the sounds of one of Pushkin's poems, his favorite writers being precisely Pushkin and Gogol.) Jokingly claiming the right to be "bitter-sounding," he, like Khlebnikov and Mayakovsky, deformed classical meters, attempting with his rhythmical "shifts" to create a poetry of intonation and accent (with a "stress on sound," on poetry as *declamation*).

"Hand on heart" (to use an expression dear to Boris Pasternak), I think it is unnecessary today to continue the argument in favor of Kruchonykh's *zaum*.

Let us listen to the poet himself: "*Zaum* is the original form of poetry, both in history and in individual development. What comes first is a rhythmically musical emotion, an *ur*-noise... *Zaum* is used: a) when an artist is setting out images that are still undefined (both for him and for me), b) when the speaker doesn't want to name an object, but merely hint at it... *Zaum* rouses us, sets free creative fantasy, not marring it with anything concrete..."

Kruchonykh's aspiration to the realm of "pure" sounds, freed of all relation to objects, is akin to Malevich's suprematism. "Sounds, and particularly vowels, were interpreted by Kruchonykh in the suprematist manner, as spatial and cosmic phenomena," writes the German scholar Rosemarie Ziegler. "The cosmic meanings of vowels were not invented by futurist poetics, but they were not previously motivated by the desire for the non-objective."

In this way, Kruchonykh overcame the barrier of the objective. For the viewer, this happens in the following manner: "We tear the letter out of the line, out of its single direction, and give it the possibility of free movement. (Lines are needed by civil servants and for private correspondence). As a result, we reach a third position, the disposition of the sonorous masses of letters in space, as in a suprematist painting" (letter from Malevich to M. Matyushin in 1916).

Here the aural dimension comes to the fore. Rosemarie Ziegler writes: "It is possible to stress the primacy of the aural in the reception of language and poetry, the primacy of the actual sound of speech as compared with historically conditioned written orthography.... Alongside phonetic spellings and colloquial, dialect, or other similar expressions, Kruchonykh used Georgian, Armenian, Turkish, German, and other expressions as poetic devices. The various sound combinations that characterize these languages are used by him as estranging devices, or else as *zaum* words."

Kruchonykh's universalism... His semi-dadaist opera *Victory over the Sun* (with music by Mikhail Matyushin), staged in 1913 at the same time as the tragedy *Vladimir Mayakovsky*, is still worth remembering and can serve as a theatrical discovery for today. (It was, in fact, put on in 1983 at an international festival in Munich.) When people began to talk of the birth of sound cinema, Kruchonykh published a book of film reviews and film scripts in verse – he could already see the possibility of "cine-poetry."

Kruchonykh the critic. Let us at least mention his style, his sharp, brilliant prose; his only rival in this field was one of his favorite disciples, Igor Terentyev.

Kruchonykh the publisher. In Russian book history he introduced something genuinely new with his "handmade books" – lithographic, hectographic, or even handwritten, always collaborating closely with the artists Malevich, Larionov, Goncharova, Tatlin, and Rozanova. His own books of 1916–17 using collage and pasted labels are splendid examples of the Malevich school of fine art.

The centenary of Kruchonykh's birth was celebrated in Kherson in 1986, thanks to the tireless efforts of the literary scholar S. M. Sukhoparov. In the official statement of principle published on this occasion, there is a restatement of the gist of a telegram sent by me to the organizing committee: "The latest publications on the work of A. Kruchonykh have enabled the poet and translator Gennady Aygi to place his name alongside those of such leading figures of twentieth-century European art as Khlebnikov and Malevich, Mayakovsky and Apollinaire, Breton and Picasso." Such is my conviction, and I repeat it here.

1989

Krch – 80

FOR THE EIGHTIETH BIRTHDAY OF A. E. KRUCHONYKH

o *being*
your surface
invisibly burning
from the touch of *non-being* –

crunches
creating a name for the poet:

krch

krch

krch

FEBRUARY 9, 1966

Mayakovsky

ANSWERS TO A QUESTIONNAIRE IN THE *LITERARY GAZETTE*

1

Has your attitude toward Mayakovsky changed? If so, when and how?

Since I was boy, I have been accustomed – at decisive moments in my life – to measure myself against Mayakovsky.

It was through him that I came to Pasternak in the mid-1950s, and through Pasternak's *Safe Conduct* that I discovered Baudelaire and Nietzsche.

But there was indeed a melancholy period when I "didn't feel like" reading Mayakovsky – the ten years or more following the Soviet occupation of Czechoslovakia. The general feeling of total deadlock became at this time something personal, "existential," and I kept going only thanks to Kierkegaard, Kafka, and Max Jacob.

I didn't forget Mayakovsky, but the thought of him had a bitter taste. However, this also passed and I returned to him, this time definitively, as a kind of *yardstick*, which constantly made me feel responsible to myself and demanded a "secret" artistic courage involving nobody but myself.

2

What is there in Mayakovsky's writings that doesn't leave you indifferent?

Mayakovsky has an extraordinary sense of verbal form and architectonics. One might even speak of his genius for "plastic thought." At the same time, his feelings in their extremity and their conflict are manifested with such power that they remind you of Shakespeare or Dostoevsky.

As a monumental thinker, he cannot be measured on the same scale as writer-thinkers of the élite, intellectual type, who sometimes appear more "correct" to an outside observer. Yet this mistake is constantly being made.

In view of his utterly honest, tragic integrity and his greatness, I was, and still am, attracted by almost everything in Mayakovsky. The grandiose *liturgical* quality of his long personal-confessional poems (both the early ones and "At the Top of My Voice") is akin to the Orthodox liturgical element in Mussorgsky. I also regard the poem "Good!" as a unique achievement – Russian poetry will never again see such a fresh and *active* idealism (it seems almost magical). In the context of the exhibition *A Great Utopia*, we can see what a rare phenomenon Mayakovsky's propaganda work really was, and the "ROSTA windows" have become a classic of graphic art throughout the world. Incidentally, this exhibition was badly named; the very name suggested in advance a one-sided approach. One should never confuse the eternal (real and active) ideals of humanity with utopia or utopianism. And in the exhibition there was much that has already become an *aesthetic reality* for all time – in the changed consciousness of millions of people. As an old friend of mine put it, "Malevich reached the cosmos before the cosmonauts."

The only aspect of Mayakovsky's work that leaves me cold is the agitpoems, which he coauthored with Aseev and Kirsanov. But even they are interesting from a purely linguistic-poetical point of view.

3

In what would you want to support him? Or dissuade him?

That is like asking the same question about Beethoven or Michelangelo.

There is no way I could "support" Beethoven, or dissuade him from anything.

For me, everything in Mayakovsky is equally great. He is incomparably greater than his age.

The current "evaluations" of Mayakovsky are directed from the present to the past. Whereas an ethical-aesthetic appreciation of the poet demands that we move out of the present into the future.

4

Can you imagine Mayakovsky after 1930? What would he do today?

Mayakovsky died along with the revolution ("his revolution," as he said). He is an immense symbol of the death of the *incomplete* revolution.

Perhaps we are now seeing the completing of its final stage (belated and apparently imitating *something* and *someone*, so that it seems somehow "amateurish").

As I see it, in spite of all the changes of one kind or another, there is nothing "unprecedentedly-immense" about our age. This is apparent in the gray nature of the mass of contemporary art, whether "traditional" (i.e. trivially argumentative) or "avant-garde" (i.e. trivially parodic). No one now is going to "trample on the throat of their own song" (as Mayakovsky put it); only great poets are capable of this, in the name of the great word. In my opinion, this is what Baudelaire and Norwid did.

There is *no need* for Mayakovsky in our age, much as during the Enlightenment there was no need for titanic Renaissance figures with their particular undiluted strength of religious and humanist conviction.

5

Does he have a future?

I am sure that Mayakovsky will come back and confront world culture as a great and serious ethical-aesthetic problem, involving the creation of literary form. The essence of Mayakovsky is a powerfully religious theomachy, and he will repeatedly demand the testing of the Word in its religious key, giving rise to the manifestation of its highest, most creative qualities.

JUNE 22, 1993

In Honor of a Master

FOR MALEVICH

Here,
when contemporary poetic writing, unthinkingly preserving its
ancient passion for *descriptiveness,* is busy with its interminable
inventory of the "new" world, the "technically created" world –

here,
where the triviality of words seems the one thing that exists
beneath an empty sky of Wordlessness –

here
moves the *creating* Word of Malevich-the-Poet ("the
distribution of sonorous masses") – erupting "clumsily" – "into
the expanse of the world" ("so that form should give presence
to the imagination" of it), alluding to its perfect future-*plasticity*
(the "agonizing" as Its "transitory" state) –

here,
amidst the convulsive breath of what is not spoken, the
fusions-and-blocks – of Words, or rather of Wordmeanings –
are *held* in motion – the "creative points of the Universe"
around what Creates.

MARCH 15, 1991

Kazimir Malevich

...and the fields go up to heaven
— FROM A VARIANT OF THE LITURGY

where the one guardian of work is the Father's image
there is no bowing to the circle
and plain boards call for no holy face

but from far off it seems the church's singing
henceforth knows no godparent-singers
and is built in the form of a city
unfamiliar with periods of time

so too in those years another will was creating
an order of its own self
city – page – iron – clearing – rectangle:

– simple as fire under ashes consoling Vitebsk

– in the sign of allusion Velimir was surrendered and seized

– but El he is like a line he is distant for leavetaking

– it seems a colophon for the Bible: cut – conclusion – Kharms

– on boards by others is completed
the sketch of a white coffin

and – the fields – go up – to heaven
from each – there is – a direction
to every – star

and wielding the iron end it beats
under the beggarly dawn
and the circle is closed: as if from heaven is seen
work to see as from heaven

1962

Massacre of a Silk Flag

ON THE PORTRAITS OF VLADIMIR YAKOVLEV

Imagine a man falling asleep in the presence of his interrogators. It is as if he is separating his face from himself, like a hoisted silk flag preserving a life distinct from the man. No need for events – blows will most likely fall on the flag.

Such are the portraits of Vladimir Yakovlev – either they are awaiting blows, or else they have already received them. They are connected to the artist, like secondary, "spiritual," protective faces.

Yakovlev's language is not topical, not metaphorical. The topical in art, when it is ignorant of genuine reality, uses a borrowed language. To define Yakovlev's language I shall have recourse to a comparison.

"The Scratch on the Sky," the title of one of Khlebnikov's longer poems, bestows a magical significance on sound, giving a metaphorical meaning to the sky. Let us suppose that there are other scratches and cuts on this sky. Let us imagine that we owe their appearance to a spirit that has no need for words and ideas.

I want to compare Yakovlev's art to that kind of "scratch on the sky." The stretched liquid and particles of dust that recall the gouaches of Wols seem to be waiting for the light to illuminate the scratches on his pictures. In his work, there are many, as I think of them, "stigmatic elements." The images of evil and suffering that he creates have nothing to do with folklore or allegory. His drawing and his color are direct and genuine, like the traces of suffering that mark out victims in the light of nature. They have more to say about our time than modish constructivism in life and art.

1966

Two Poems for Vladimir Yakovlev

Windows on Trubnaya Square in Spring

With swaying squares
of the flowering and ringing
of all my childhoods, familiar
to transparent deserted cities,

I touch them, and the maidenly weddings
will continue the same
without either music or doors,

the depths are glimmering
greenish – somber
and beyond them weep for them
butchers smeared in rain
fallen on heaps of fish,

and again a stamping and a stepping – I am here, I am here,

a stamping and a stepping – once and for ever – like a bell in mist –
and like – titles – of akathists –
I dream – of a red – separation – and meeting

1961

Good Mornings:
On Vladimir Yakovlev's Painting "Black Flower"

TO A. I. PEVZNER

let it long remain
turned toward you
black mysterious Guardian
severe and elegant
flower –

accompanying from morning
to your little table
the different shadows –

wreaths of quietist
patriarchal ponds –

trembling in air

APRIL 9, 1963

An Evening with Shalamov

I first read Shalamov in the summer of 1965. I was sitting by myself in the empty basement of a painter friend, and there was a pile of typewritten pages on the table. I began to read them – it was "The Green Prosecutor" of Varlam Shalamov.

I don't like the word "shattered" – it's an overused word. What happened to me was something different; a kind of *mighty, heavy tread* invaded me, my space, my destiny... the powerful steps of Great Prose, unprecedented in the Russian prose of our time.

I have never liked the lively, fragmented, showy prose that came into modern Russian literature (as Boris Pasternak rightly stated) with Andrey Bely and his narcissistic genius for the sentence (a unique phenomenon, which demands a special approach, irrespective of its consequences). Mikhail Bulgakov's *Master and Margarita* leaves me cold – for me it is "literature" (in Verlaine's sense: "everything else is literature"); I don't like Nabokov's prose (it remains a "firework" for me, and I feel only the "appropriate" reaction to *Lolita*). Until I read Andrey Platonov's *Foundation Pit* (which seems to me to put Platonov on a level with Joyce, Céline, and Kafka), I could not know that the "effects" of his style came from the agonizing quest for a new direction (a direction of genius) in Russian literature.

I sensed in "The Green Prosecutor" a kind of special, previously nonexistent *great form* of prose (not a novel, an investigation, a *novella*... but something abstractly-pure and weighty, corresponding to the "non-fictional" tragedy of the age).

In the summer of 1967, I wrote a poem, "Degree: Of Stability," which I dedicated to Shalamov (the Russian word for stability here, *ostoika*, is a term derived from *ostoichivost*, a naval term for the stability of a vessel).

That December, I got a phone call from my close friend Konstantin Bogatyryov: "Come this evening to the Rozhansky's – they are expecting your favorite author."

I am still grateful to I. D. Rozhansky and N. V. Kind for the long evening I was able to spend in their apartment with Varlam Shalamov – my only meeting with him.

It was a very difficult evening for all of us. From time to time we would all go silent, as if we were in the presence of "someone" – a man Emerged-from-Hell... – there's no other way of putting it.

I have noticed on various occasions that former inmates of the camps (*zeks*), when they first make one another's acquaintance, immediately "recognize" one another and establish a special form of communication that remains in some respects taboo for outsiders.

Konstantin Bogatyryov, generally a very sociable person, made some discreet and delicate, but still *zek*-like, attempts to start up a conversation with a *zek* who was his senior. Shalamov immediately made it clear (in some inexplicable way, without a gesture, a look, or a word) that this was impossible. (In a numb wordlessness, it was as if these silence-"words" reared up: "I come from a place where you have not been.")

Rozhansky suggested that Shalamov should record some readings on a tape recorder. Shalamov was happy with this: he wanted to read his poems. Two or three quiet voices were heard: "Couldn't you read some of your prose?" Varlam Tikhonovich read a story, I can't remember which one. And at this point something occurred during his reading that increased our general feeling of numbness (may I be forgiven for having to say this): the writer suddenly began to gesticulate with a kind of "twitching" and began speaking very quickly... and ... no doubt it's better not to try to describe our impressions or to discuss the "impact" of such language as compared with ordinary speech.

Varlam Tikhonovich sensed this feeling of numbness. He looked at us rapidly with his anthracite-hard eyes and swiftly took control of himself. Once again, we were in the presence of a harmonious, artistic person with easy movements; his hands were not "bordering on the beautiful," but simply beautiful (many people, when they first saw the writer at his funeral service at the church of St. Nicholas of the Smiths, were amazed at the beauty of his hands).

I shall take the liberty of saying directly ("this is how it was") that on that evening I could feel that same *heavy tread* that I had heard in the unforgettable "Green Prosecutor."

I attempted (twice, as I recall) to tell Varlam Tikhonovich about the impression I had received much earlier from that work, and from his prose in general. He remained silent. Then he said a few words, without any special intonation: "I have been thinking about prose all my life, and I know I have found the right form for what I write."

At this point Konstantin Bogatyryov joined politely in the conversation: "In one story you write 'four kilometers.' But was the distance perhaps slightly different in reality, three kilometers, say, or five?"

"If I said 'four', it was four," Shalamov replied. "In all I have written, everything was exactly as I described it."

Konstantin asked Shalamov how he felt about *Doctor Zhivago*. Again there was a brief answer with no special intonation: "*Safe Conduct, Lyuvers' Childhood*, 'A Tale' – these are works of genius. Such prose only appears once in two hundred years."

I cite these three moments during our evening with Shalamov because I think they show that in spite of his rather exaggerated opinion of his verse, he had long known very clearly what he was aiming for in his prose.

From 1965 on, I had occasion to hear from very thoughtful people with a good knowledge of literature that Shalamov's prose was simply "factography," little more than "sketches." I always tried to show them how behind this "factographic prose" there was a great Poet and a great Artist, that almost everything he wrote was permeated with a *specifically poetic* way of seeing and thinking, that of a true master; this penetrated the text like a powerful light, with no affected mystery. (Remember his favorite *stlanik* – a low growing but tenacious conifer – that spreads not with its roots but with its tragic rays throughout his work; remember the *graphite,* which marks not only the notches in the trees and the *identification tags* on the feet of the dead *zeks*, but also our souls, our memory, and our altered perception of the "aesthetic.")

One of my friends – after a seventeen-year argument – only came to agree completely with my opinions about Shalamov the artist when he read all the Kolyma tales in one large volume. Varlam Tikhonovich proved to have been tragically right when he protested at the piecemeal publication of his writings.

The first person to note this tragedy was Mikhail Geller, to whom Russian literature owes the most complete – and careful – edition of Shalamov's prose. Among literary critics, the best evaluation of Shalamov's works, as I see it, was given by Andrey Sinyavsky alone, in a quite remarkable radio broadcast of 1981.

Thinking of Shalamov's prose, I used to remember one of my early impressions of Kafka.

It so happened that I got to know Kafka's very first stories only after I had read everything of his that had been published in French translation (including the letters and the diaries). At first I felt disappointed by the early stories, since the artificial, "Hoffmannesque" devices were so obvious in them; the youthful Kafka was doing violence to his work so as to communicate some "mysterious essence."

However, it was precisely these early works that "demonstrated" to me the immense and agonizing labor through which Kafka attained the *simplicity of a new language*, and that the miracle of this simplicity engendered the most mysterious and essential works of the epoch.

I believe that Varlam Shalamov achieved this kind of *simplicity* in his own way. There is no work in which the *tragic element* in the recent history of our people is rendered in a language as appropriate to this lofty tragedy as that of the great Book of the author of the *Kolyma Tales*.

In the course of this evening with Varlam Tikhonovich, I was often reminded of a well-known saying about "people who have died to life while still alive." I was absorbed in watching Shalamov the artist. What happened subsequently showed that a poet, even one "Emerged-from-Hell," can still have a weakness; there is still something *living* in him – in relation to Poetry.

I told Varlam Tikhonovich that one of my poems was dedicated to him. This interested him greatly. Telling me straight away that "there wasn't an absolute need for us to meet," he said that his friend I. S. would come and collect the poem from me. He continued to show a lively interest in the promised poem; I couldn't meet I. S. straight away, and she phoned several times to say that Varlam Tikhonovich had again reminded her about the poem. I wanted him to read this poem dedicated to him alongside other poems of mine; in other words, in the context of my poetics, which was after all very different from the "generally accepted" poetic language of the period.

Having received a typescript of my poems, Shalamov replied very speedily. By way of I. S. he sent me a copy of his book of poems entitled *Road and Fate* with the dedication: "To the poet Gennady Lisin [my former name], with deep sympathy. I do not believe in free verse, but I believe in poetry! V. Shalamov. Moscow, January 1968."

What he had not openly said in the dedication was conveyed to me from the author by I. S.: "I do not believe in free verse. I have never believed it can be poetry," repeated Shalamov, "but strangely enough, this is free verse, and it is poetry."

Thanking me for the dedicatory poem, he asked I. S. to tell me word for word: "A lot has been written about me, in poetry, even in a song. I don't like any of it. This poem is the best that has been written about me, the only thing that faithfully reflects me and my work."

On that evening at the Rozhanskys we left together at midnight. In the hall, Varlam Tikhonovich struggled for a long time to put on his coat: he was trying to use his right hand (which was already "dressed") to stick his left hand into the sleeve. I made a movement to help him, but he flashed me a stern, even a harsh look.

So I was all the more surprised when on parting he suddenly bowed and with an "elegant" movement (there is no other word for it) rapidly took the hand of the young woman who was with me, pressed it to his lips ("All the best") and left us equally rapidly.

My contact with Varlam Tikhonovich continued by way of I. S. On several occasions, he sent some new (concluding) pages of the *Kolyma Tales* for me to read.

Once, having noticed that in the stories there were occasional minor flaws (repetition of the same phrase in two different tales; use of the first person in a story told in the third person), I took the liberty of telling the author through I. S. that a "negligible" amount of editing was called for, and that if he agreed I could, with the greatest respect for the work, take this on myself. His answer was short (but, as I. S. conveyed it to me, "not lacking a bitter intonation"): "It's all the same to me. These are trifles. They can be sorted out later. The main thing for me is to have time to tell a truth that no one in the world knows about."

I remained under the enormous influence of Shalamov's works for some fifteen years. Throughout this period, in a whole series of my poems, there are variations on images and "motifs" which appeared as a result of the tragic spirit of his writings.

MARCH 10, 1982

Degree: Of Stability

TO V. SHALAMOV

You yourself are already visited by something like skyglow:

and the image perhaps
has become real for all:

independent of all:

is this not the unseen flame of poverty
in the noiseless wind:

of the shortlived features? –

or possibility of the perilous i t i s:

in faces illumined –

as if waiting
to be opened:

like those who guard something? –

or – with un-clear incandescence (as if staring with a kind of
    vision of unhurried illness):

everywhere – unseen – illuminating all:

the ultimate i t
of the Fire-Word:

which long ago seized
the very places of our thoughts? –

has it everywhere as in a noiseless wind:

without word without spirit:

itself come into being?

1967

II.

THE WIDER WORLD

O Yes: Light of Kafka

1

Last summer my sister went to Prague. I asked her to visit the old cemetery of the city and to lay a "Moscow" stone on Kafka's grave for me. (I knew this was what Jews used to do when visiting graves that were dear to them.)

The day after my sister carried out my request, a Prague lady expressed a desire to meet her. The word "shock" is one I have never used in relation to myself. But this was exactly what I felt when I found out *who* this woman was.

"The daughter of... Ottla?" I kept repeating, "The daughter... of Ottla? Is it possible?"

Kafka, his sisters, Auschwitz, his sisters' husbands, ash, almost all of his family, a photograph of Kafka before my eyes with his beloved sister, ash and the smoke of Auschwitz, and suddenly, in the light of a Moscow day, this simple "the daughter of Ottla?" – and my sister's words: "She knows your name and she sends you her regards."

Once I had recovered, I said, "I feel as if I had touched the sleeve of a saint."

In my desk drawer, there is a chestnut leaf from *his* grave and a white stone – *from the same place...* – it is only very rarely that I allow myself to touch them.

And now I am venturing to touch the name of Kafka, which is sacred to me (I can find no other way of saying it). I want to say something about him simply because I can hear these words of his niece: "I know all the articles that have been published about my uncle in your country, but I don't know how ordinary readers feel about him."

2

I know people whose faces shine with a certain expression, a certain *wordless purity* – and I know how that expression is fully tried and tested – in the world of Kafka's visions.

Such people recognize one another by this strange "Kafka-like" luminosity of the face, just as one believer recognizes, *senses* another believer.

I am not claiming to be one of these people – not to that degree. I simply want to say that there are such readers of Kafka in Russia.

But one must also mention another type of reader. "How terrible!" is a quite understandable reaction. But "How gloomy!"– how often I have also heard that reaction to Kafka's work (and in all our literary criticism I know only one article that does not degrade his character or seek out "failings" in his work).

There is another common approach to Kafka that could be called the search for "truth in a can."

A goner in a prison camp picks up an empty can on the perimeter and scrapes around in it for the tiniest scrap of something to eat – thus the expression I have just used (it was given me by a now deceased Russian priest).

There are readers who seem almost to take pleasure in searching in Kafka for crumbs of "truth" in the form of "hints"; whereas in Kafka there is the beginning of an almost trans-existential "space." Is there not beyond his "existential" torment the gleam of something whole – not fragmented simply so that "people can understand it" – and does not this unfragmented whole confront us invisibly, concentrating all our attention, our secret being, in an extreme tension, a responsible wholeness, as if we were looking into *something* into which, as we well know, one cannot look?

Kafka is beyond Allegory, beyond Symbol – these gates of the universal human Temple have already closed behind him. He is "somewhere," in an invisible Concentration that is unconcealed yet inaccessible – but even so we seem-to-see-and-hear Him.

We say "the Apophatic" – from the impossibility of speaking – but does it consist simply of *darkness*? And we seem to hear something like an inexpressibly-painful human refrain (about "those who sing in the heavens"): *light*, how then did you come to be – *displaced*?... – how did you – in your oneness – become hidden from souls (of light-and-of-darkness) – together with the darkness?

3

Once I was very surprised by Akhmatova (who is usually so clear-sighted) – by a line of hers spoken on the radio (with the "Voice" of somewhere): "Such a thing Kafka might have invented."

But Kafka *invented* nothing. He *saw*.

And what people see is not darkness; with inner human light they see another *Inner Light*.

Even Auschwitz doesn't consist only of darkness *(even such a thing* we cannot imagine otherwise): there is a cry of *light* (invisible, "unheard-of" – yes, we ask: was the Apophatic not

split open – in some "mystical time" – in some kind of "repetition"?
– we do not know these "times," we know our own time, when
Some-Thing-like-that has indeed been split open). Were there
ever such *scorched* faces? Is radiation (God forgive me) not a
pitiful caricature (something second-hand, third-hand) of the
splitting open in time of the Times?

But it is extremely difficult for us to "determine" (and if we
"guess at" something, it is impossible to speak it) What or Who
is concerned with this *light*... – undoubtedly the light of the
Terrible, only not in "our sense," but the Terrible-in-Itself, as in
the torments of the Unrevealed-at-a-time-of-Necessary-
Revelation. But who, however "knowledgeable" they may be,
can affirm that Creation is already complete? – are we not
situated *within* some *tragic* stage of its continuation?

A baby is pure (there are depths beyond the reach of "classic
Freudianism" or any of its variants), its purity perceives a great
deal that is inaccessible to us; and does not this *innocent wisdom*,
this *holy wisdom* perceive the *inner light* of the world in a way
that cannot be communicated to us in our common language,
whereas it is possible to talk with us *in such a way* that within
this conversation, inseparable from it, is the terrifying shining
of the inexpressible, and we can at least *feel* that?

4

The incredible purity of Kafka is such that one can say to
people (and there are such people around me): "Don't touch
Jewish blood, maybe that's enough" (I must stress that I am
thinking simply of *blood-as-liquid*).

What a strange common characteristic of the Trio – Kafka,
Jacob, Celan: to slide along the razor's edge of the name of

Unnamed, provoking fear that at any minute a blasphemous word will be spoken, but no – the blade simply becomes brighter; where is the blood?... – here is blood-as-silence, and the cry is *light*, which is greater than hope and despair, and that light is the presence... of what? – of the most Real... – as if this were the splitting of the self-radiation of what is more serious than the "dialectical" nucleus made of the unity of "the-terrible-and-the-not-terrible," – oh, this again – and with inconceivable Closure! – and does not something of this radiation reach us (for something responds in us – is it not so? – to this "something" that reaches us... What more can we say?).

5

We forget, then remember (and this is the "succession of times," so we live-and-abide); we do not want to remind ourselves that there is something more serious than the terrible. Such, for example, is the light from the depths, hidden, elusive, and persistent, not only in Kafka's *Castle*, not only in his "Mole," but even in his "Eleven Sons."

In his unparalleled book *Conversations with Kafka* (perhaps the agonizing purity of Kafka is expressed even more intensely in the record of his words preserved in this book than in his own diaries), Gustav Janouch tells how when the word "God" was spoken, Kafka remained silent, "as if he had gone away somewhere." But in speaking of Kafka, we cannot avoid using this word. "God" or "He" is more serious than this word without inverted commas.

I can say that before this palely and darkly shining face – the image of Kafka – I know that I would always use this word – because of my powerlessness to express what exists but is resistant to any form of "explanation." Once, having written down the letters of this previously taboo word-concept, I said of it that "He" was more powerful than good (and that is the point: that it is wasn't more powerful than "good and evil." "More powerful than good" – that is where it lies, the terrible – so it is better just to say of it: "more powerful than good").

I am deliberately not saying anything here about Kafka's "labyrinths of the Absurd" – enough has already been written about this, and in any case there is something more than the "Absurd" in Kafka.

And that is what has happened: here, in these pages, I am a prisoner of *tautologies,* which all express the same radiance – a strange radiance? – yes, like everything in Kafka; oh *this face* – I knew that it would inevitably draw me into the whirlpool of a kind of probing operating-theater whiteness.

Aleksandr Solzhenitsyn once remarked that "literature is not the barking of dogs in a village." Yes indeed – and it is also not marketplace shouting or lawcourt wrangling. It is when, without any narration or description ("nothing concrete"), we are struck by the light of the Essential... – how does that happen? "But he writes all that with the language of an ABC," an acquaintance of mine (a remarkable musician) once said about Kafka. Yes, that is true... – but if, by way of this ABC language, something fantastically unified and ominous reaches us, this means that there is some sort of "intermediate language" radiating a light of such "poverty," as if we were in the presence of a *terrible simplicity* – of some kind of miracle, of the *miracle itself!...* – and again I want to say that this undefined language is the unrepeatable *light of Kafka.*

When one hears the words "work of art," one should immediately ask what it means in this particular case: a *discovery*, or a *composition*? The former is expressed in an undemonstrable but *present* light of revelation – the uncovering of the *essence of the tragic*. Composition circles around feebly putting together ponderous descriptions, reflections, contrived "fantasmogorias" (and how, from their inability to look straight into the light of Day of our times, into the vividly multi-inclusive terrible things in the light of this Day, our contemporary *littérateurs* have rushed into innumerable interpretations of the myths "of all times and all peoples"). Oh how all this is accumulated and compiled in the hope that something will shine forth out of this great heap – thanks to the multitude of "demonstrations" and "illustrations." But the *light of discovery* is absent; there is an endless shuffling of contrived situations, the work puffs up with excess of composition – how "significant" they are, these currently rather numerous "Invitations to a Beheading" and their variants ("they try to frighten me, but I am not afraid") – how "rich" these books are compared to the "poor" novels of Kafka.

The language of the tragic changes; one cannot speak of new horrors in the old language. The "abnormal" Russian language in Platonov's *Foundation Pit* (what *displacements* of words – how can a "literate Russian writer" construct a sentence like that?), his truly strange, in some ways otherworldly-alogical, syntax creates first and foremost a *new atmosphere* of the tragic (whose language had already changed "in the heavens" sooner than among us). The writer does not describe "as it is" the unfolding of its consequences. Moreover, even within "what is" there have been displacements – Platonov's language, the shudder caused by the shudder of his inner being, closely follows these secret displacements.

"Truth in art is incandescence" – this sentence from an old unfinished poem keeps ringing in my head. And I want to say it again here, without any further explanation.

6

And this K. is moving among us (he is not only the hero of two novels – this branding-letter could replace the characters' names in a whole series of Kafka stories), he is wandering, K.... – a strange figure no doubt, but in what way?

He would be less than the "living," if we were keeping awake in the name of the familiar slogan: "one has to live"(but why this "has to"?), if we were such "full-blooded people," it would be better to keep away from us.

He is also less than the "full-blooded" figures from the novels of the nineteenth century (or rather of previous centuries), but we are not genuinely awake; we cannot wake into Vigilance-Life, and he wanders among us, this K., who is bigger – and more real – than we are.

And he moves on – in that illumination whose name is the Vigilance of the tormented perspicacity of Kafka; isn't the word "life" sometimes the tautological equivalent of the idea of a *herd mentality*? – and Kafka's "parables" are like an indirect light at a distance from this amorphous fog; but if we achieve wakefulness in blazingly-pitiless Concentration of Day, then any of Kafka's "parables" can occupy the central point of this Concentration; and what is more, we do not dwell so dimly in a drowsy absence of spiritual attention – even that very absence is now like the sky-glow of an all-human alarm ("not-ness" is a particular light) and in it, not as a shadow, but as a distant, irrevocable deep sky-glow, sliding and flickering, wanders K.

"Such solitude is still not enough – one must be even more alone," said Max Jacob. Such solitude has not been given to me.

Years passed by, and my despair turned inside out, showing its *lining* – the "affirmation of life" – is that not the way it was? – yes, and it is not for nothing that I sometimes feel ashamed when confronted by the name of Kafka.

I have lost the purity of solitude and the chastity of being unknown (even so, I knew something of this chastity). I wanted to be "necessary," but what quiet happiness and honesty there is in being *unnecessary*! These are the "lessons of Kafka" (I remember, I still remember only very little), that is the only reason for my saying "I" here – at one time this "I" was tested, penetrated by the light of Kafka. Yes, he was so dear to me, for many years, in my poems, I wrote about him not with any "literary intention" – I talked with him in the purity of Solitude, his Solitude, in which I sometimes found room for my own beggarly-contracted, poor-and-silent condition, knowing how turbid it seemed before the light of Kafka.

I could say to my holy Brother (how could he mean less to me than some of my beloved "canonized" saints?), I could say to him one thing only: "I was trying to say something, without a listener.... It went on like that for a long time.... I never knew who I was talking to, it was happiness 'in the Word'.... Without You, I should never have retained my faith and patience in the name of the Word.... I proved unworthy of the breath of that 'subtle cold,' and even so, before your Pure Name, I can say – I knew it."

I fall silent – again there is before me the sleeve (seeming white as snow) of the Saint – I am afraid to touch it.

SEPTEMBER 27–NOVEMBER 7, 1985

For a Conversation about K. –
To Olga Mashkova

earth is just a thought – freely visiting:

changing:

sometimes known to me
in a thought that is Prague:

and then I see
a grave in the city –

it is like a grief-thought:

earth – of suffering!... his – as of that thought
which is now so constant!...

I shall say of that grave "a dream":

and – as even wounds do not make us believe it is real –

he seems dreamed
in another sleep:

as if unending:

by me

1967

Reading Norwid

WINTER NOTES
To W. W.

1

in the light of gladness (forgive me brothers of Norwid)
I grow dark with the shades of words: "Janowska Street"
as a D e a t h – b r i g a d e myself in my own soul
I seem to move onward more blackly

2

and like one dead I am glad you are among the living

3

D e a t h – b r i g a d e – sky above the super-Place
now girlish laughter – as over you the hand
smeared with poison of the dead
a baby's babbling – reflection of day
on forehead and on eyes – as if in pieces
in the R a v i n e – W o r l d of the pseudo-living
and you are one of those: living moving along
with half-putrefaction smearing others

4

when Grief-should-long ago-have-been-among-the-corpses
when it-is-Time-to-abandon-the Province of the living

5

and you brothers of the T w e n t i e t h   P r e l u d e!
through the sleep of the world
in the last drop of reason
your   a n c h o r   above you
is shining – become: the last-body-of-the-Day
(ever more – my-body too!)
let me remember no other! and in going
not to shine another Word
laying waste – with no place now – the drop

6

O this Turnedawayness-Turbulence yes centerless contentless –
O God is it into the-gap-Powązki – O with the circle the long
darkened circle – yes speed without strength – O more already
without itself ever more without and including such things:
without it already the piano the blizzard Powązki and the voice
– without Frycek the voice beneath heaven with no other
heaven – there will be no other when this world without a
people Powązki

and there is only One heaven – beneath it Dead-Without-Meaning
shakes the Daisy of Socialist Fraternity:
the same Guessing Game: "will they won't they"

again – of Chopin t o u s!   what John
with what power
and what fire
will transform t h o s e s o u n d s – into what? – so the World-as-Shame
should blaze (and here – any over-word!)
of Chopin – t o u s! – is it not? – to the tribe
of such (it was spoken) a super-Place

when it is Time-High-Time-to-be-among-the-corpses
when it is Time-to-be-leaving-the-Province-of-the-living

but brothers the light when you are gladness brothers
and the truth is this: they do not share the shining
but they gleam (and somewhere: "you have to keep living")
while the dead "when" of others
is no more than the corpse of the whisper "when"

11

and with this a discovery: t h e y
it turns out are able to squeak
when you tread on their p a r t y – c o r n s
(and will the d i s c o v e r y become a w e a p o n)
....
(for werewolves with a werewolf echo
like a revelation of o r i g i n s
such materialism is being made ready)
....
....

12

when it is Grief-to-be-among-the-corpses-Grief
in space be c r a s h – o f – t h e – c r a s h e s "O Muse"

13

but we also understood the a d v a n t a g e
of a prison like that: the more the better
(it was – but it turned out: not for us)
and what now is there for us – the brotherly-Abandoned
by our own d e p a r t e r s?
the less the prison the worse

14

the degrees of Its definition
you seem not-to-have-read-no! – and in the Deadness of Silence
I mutter (or wordlessly shudder)
I repeat them with self-in-tatters-of-darkness:
Gas-Chamber-Land – Foul-Weather-Land
Suffocation-Land and Land-all-is-finished

15

when it is Grief-to-be-among-corpses-Grief
when it is Time-to-be-leaving-the-Province-of-the-living

1980

Baudelaire

It was not you who killed not you who defeated
it was not of your field

Not for nothing you could not hear him
something from somewhere dictated
not having a place of its own

and there were not it seemed either lips brows or temples
other than the distant voice
and the unexpected hands

And even the laws of movement and growth
sought another way of serving him:

that place beneath heaven was unforeseen
where all was ratified as gravity

and from everyone this gravity separated him
as something falling
is separated from air in air

– and his eyes the color of Spanish tobacco
were alive before death
and longing for the purity

that is born of rupture and ruin alone

1957

O Yes: The Smile of Max Jacob

PREFACE TO A CYCLE OF POEMS

1

Something was shifting, it seemed, something existed and within it – from time to time – something caught fire. But even this seemed to come from the "other world."

It seemed that even Hell and Satan were now worn down by the Tedium of this time and this place (I used to call it "super-Place," transposing the shameless expression "superpower").

It was like the death of Death itself – and we, were we alive? did we "resist"? More likely, we were simply *there*, in this "transfigured, newly manifested" death, and perhaps there was nothing we could say about this "time."

2

And whose faces do I remember, whose eyes?

Only those of a few people whom I inwardly (for myself) called the "witnesses of truth" – to use an expression of Søren Kierkegaard.

Those who "wrote philosophy" (as professionals), even when they were among the "witnesses," could not, as I saw it, reveal to me something "ultimate" – some kind of frighteningly-truthful *light* – in the indefinable "fissure" within a human being (or rather, within a few – separate – human beings).

3

As I write these words I can see Kafka's face, with its veiled ambiguous expression – suddenly, for the first time, it seemed to me that this face would have been an attractive "subject" for Leonardo – say, for the canvas where, as we know, the *cross* appeared in St. John's hand only after the picture had been finished – in the final stage of work.

4

I always imagine Max Jacob smiling, and I love his smile. Perhaps it is a deceptively soft smile? The way he managed to remain on the edge of a kind of blasphemy, managed to stay there, abide there in thought, vision, and the song of words – on a knife's edge, shining with its light, grieving, pulsating, lasting.

5

But still, it was a *kindly* smile. Warm as bread. Living as the silence of a tree. And indeed I have quite often written for *him* (as for Nerval and Kafka). Thanks to him (and particularly to his posthumous *L'Homme de cristal*), I twice managed to reach a state of such *incandescence* in myself that I "naturally" was able to call Him "Tu."

And – I will not describe the poems printed here as *trifles*. Whatever they might be, they rustle for me in that winter darkness of the city limits, where – if I think back to it – two yellowish stains immediately start crackling – two dogeared books of his *Le Cornet à dès.*

And – hearing Jacob's "Try to keep your prickles," I clearly – even now – smile – the bush all bare and battered, but still "standing firm."

6

On leaving Saint-Benoît (which I had visited with my Paris friends in December 1988), I also took my leave of the river Loire, which flowed like a consoling whisper – I had never seen such a "full-watered" river ("my" Volga, in my native Chuvash land, has long been disfigured beyond recognition by "man-made seas") and it seemed that a slight breath, a slight whisper of the wind might splash a drop of water onto the bank – as onto a face – and so, with just such a drop of gratitude-and-grief, I say goodbye to this book (and in some measure, to the smile of Max Jacob).

MOSCOW
OCTOBER 21, 1994

René Char

Gennady Nikolaevich, how would you characterize in a few words your creative relations with René Char over the last twenty years?

I have been corresponding with Char since 1968. On the publication of my Chuvash-language anthology, *Poets of France from the Fifteenth to the Twentieth Century*, René Char was the first person to respond. In order to do this, he copied out the publisher's address in Cyrillic script, rather awkwardly it is true, and thank goodness, this precious postcard reached me. The mere fact that the first to write to me was France's greatest contemporary poet moved me deeply. Writing back to thank him, I told Char that I had difficulty getting hold of his books and only possessed a few isolated volumes of his. And he began sending me all his publications, and other things besides – he often sent me pictures of his native Provence, of Avignon and the Vaucluse, and we began to correspond regularly. I addressed him as "Maître"; I felt myself to be in some ways his follower, and I once told him so directly. He always replied in words of rare precision, and these replies buoyed me up in periods of black despair, when I seemed to be struck dumb, surrounded by a deathly silence. What is more, I gradually came to feel a desire on his part to associate me with his country, with Provence and his beloved Sorgue, which came to take on a symbolic resonance for me. I felt that he was making me a gift of his homeland. So now, in losing him, I have lost not only a favorite poet, but a friend and teacher. A friend who having sensed a kind of confusion in my feelings, once wrote to me, "Let us thank life for sometimes being less demanding of us than people usually think." How often I felt happy and at ease with life and the world when I remembered these wise words of my beloved "distant interlocutor"!

What attracts you to René Char's poetry?

In recent decades, or more precisely in the whole period since World War II, there has been – quite logically, perhaps – a decline of the Word as humanity's most essential possession. The Word has begun to degenerate and has lost its significance as the preeminent creative force; in our day, generally speaking, poetry has gradually been transformed into sheer rhetoric and a self-contained game of "literature," and we have seen a cult of contempt for life and for the world as such, and then a cult of despair – or in reality, pseudo-despair, since this calculated "despair" served as the basis for solid worldly careers.

In this contemporary world, where the word has degenerated so much, I cannot name a poet who has steadfastly and over a whole lifetime maintained the dignity and greatness of the Poetic Word as René Char has. He was a great stoic, but a man of more than one dimension; even this word "stoic" once produced the following reaction from him: "To be a Stoic is to freeze into immobility and to wear the beautiful mask of Narcissus." He tended to reject the very possibility of a self-definition of this kind, and in this sense his spiritual struggle was at the highest level: whenever he achieved anything, he seemed immediately to begin struggling with himself and splitting himself along the line of truth; he showed immense vigilance on behalf of the struggling spirit.

René Char is a hermetic, difficult poet, but in France he had an established reputation – he was a kind of patriarch. As you see it, how compatible are poetic hermeticism and the appeal to a wide circle of readers?

The interconnection between the Word and life, in the case of René Char, was always a strange one. He exerted a continuous influence on the whole of European poetry, an influence that was both overt and secret. It seems to me that his secret influence was much greater. And his poetry undoubtedly contains a great secret, which we associate with the term "hermeticism." When readers stop respecting the Word and take no account of it, then the Word exercises its own self-respect, it becomes proud in the good sense of the word: *it does not shut itself away*, but acquires a still greater dignity in itself. It is as if the Poetic Word was saying, "It's not a question of whether you want to know me or not. But if you do want to know me, you must be prepared to engage in something very serious." I think that so-called "hermeticism" is a kind of trust in the human being, in the *creative* human being who becomes a co-creator, a co-poet. If René Char is read very attentively, he never leaves the reader without a light, without the gift of special illumination, without a new wisdom even. And the fact that such a personality and such a poet, constantly seen as "hermetic," should have possessed great popularity (*narodnost*) and even become an object of national pride in his lifetime, is explicable, as I see it, by the fact that over the last half-century or more the conception of *narodnost* in literature has changed radically. It is not the same thing as accessibility, or rhetorical "clarity" for a wide circle of readers; it is rather (and René Char's work seems to me a proof of this) a complex light from the deep roots of ethics and aesthetics, fused together with the sources of national culture, which are still perceptible if one can only retain the memory of them and discover in oneself a fidelity to them.

In my view, René Char's work is unique in demanding that we pose and resolve the problem of popularity (*narodnost*) in poetry in a new way, with a new depth and on a new creative basis.

You also addressed René Char in poetry. For instance, there is a poem of 1970 dedicated to him...

Yes, that is the poem titled "Field: In the Full Blaze of Winter." I have already mentioned that over the years of our correspondence Char "gave" me various aspects of his native land. In this poem of 1970, I did what I could to present René Char, my favorite French poet, with the face of my country – this was the only gift I could give him, and the most precious.

MARCH 6, 1988

Field: In the Full Blaze of Winter

TO RENÉ CHAR

god-pyre! – this open field
letting all things pass through (mile-posts and wind and distant
specks of mills: all more and more – as if from this world –
not in waking – gathering distance: oh all these are sparks –
not rending the flame of the pyre-that-is-not-of-this-universe)
"I am" – without trace of anything whatever
not-of-this-universe shining
god-pyre

1970

On the Poetry of Tomas Tranströmer

1

In Russia poets still "sing" (quite often they "howl" – I am speaking of the way they "deliver" their compositions). In Europe they seem to lecture or at best, they have a conversation, albeit one-sided, with their audience.

Tomas Tranströmer's work can help us to find (as Velimir Khlebnikov put it) the "true angle of the heart" for dealing with this "fait accompli" in modern poetry.

A specific inner melos (no doubt the wordless expression of the traditions – the secret traditions – of the fathers of the people) apparently no longer operates in poetry. (It's the same *everywhere* – we too are "coming to this.")

It seems to me that Tranströmer's clear, direct language, like the cold light of the northern sky, draws us into itself, gradually and unnoticeably. We have here a quite different "magic" and "enchantment" (they exist, though, they are real, even if I put the words in quotes).

The laconism, and indeed the harmony of a new artistic plenitude, are controlled here by the passionate attentiveness and the restrained humanity of the man who speaks. Spirituality is concealed under the appearance of descriptiveness (an "object world" that has long been filled with suffering and compassion – "the tug-boat rusts, putting down roots on dry land; in the earth you can hear groaning and sobbing...").

As I am drawn into this poetry, I hear a strange "non-obligatory" monologue, this conversation seems to be "with no one"; it is skeptical – so as not to seem like words of wisdom (and in reality it is just that, wise), feeling seems to be excluded, but look more closely and you find a concealed, fragile feeling – as in the lines about a man – about the poet himself – "borne by his shadow, like a violin in a case."

"God," in this poetry, "is not dead." This world gleams with the cold light of a constantly present *abandonment...by whom?* There is no need even to ask this question – when Tranströmer's poems end and fall silent, they continue to act on us with a persistent silence.

"Everything turned out much more complicated," I say to myself as I write these lines. The clarity and simplicity of the verse are deceptive – no, the word "deceptive" is wrong here, given what I see as the unique honesty and genuineness of Tranströmer's art.

It would be truer to say that this poetry is illuminated by a powerful poetic spirit, and by the rare quality of the poet himself (...a radiant figure – knowing this from personal experience, I can allow myself to use this word).

2

This poetry is a kind of "discipline" for the spirit. It is communicative without condescension and personal without the literary "personalism" that is all too common today.

And in the world of this poetry any object, any concept seems ready to split apart from its inner contradictions. The polysemic nature of Tranströmer's metaphors (which are regularly described by scholars as "exceptional" and "remarkable") seems to come from some kind of spectral disintegration; there is a constant dark flicker of paradox – but I personally see a light even in the depths of this darkness, the light of the kind soul of a great poet and a great person – and perhaps it is the combination of these qualities that gives his lyrics their unique quality and makes them known throughout the world.

Life is the fulfilment of one single duty, that of existing. It is not a question of "joy," but of that mysterious and demanding element which surpasses our powers but "in some strange way" corresponds to them. As he fulfils this duty, the poet Tranströmer experiences keenly and with the same intensity both the sufferings of the earth and of nature and humanity's inalienable poverty – like the hospital visions that haunt him (he is by profession a psychiatrist and a doctor for the handicapped).

We first began to hear of Tranströmer in 1976. In the April issue of *Questions of Literature*, there was a fine detailed article by E. Golovin about the forty-year-old poet, a memorable evocation of "the solitary inhabitant of a hut in the middle of the Swedish forests." Even as a major contemporary poet who has traveled throughout the world, he remains faithful to his "province" and to the unassuming – and possibly in some ways "undemanding" – life of solitude.

In the meantime, it seems to me that Russian poetry has long needed the infusion of something from the lyrics of Tomas Tranströmer. To sober us down a bit, and remind us once more of something that is "ours" – and Tyutchev's – "be courageous... keep up the struggle."

1994

For a Long Time:
Into Whisperings and Rustlings

ONCE MORE — IN MEMORY OF PAUL CELAN

Whisperings, rustlings. As if wind were penetrating into a cold storeroom and flour scattering somewhere. Or – straw trembling in a yard abandoned by all. The rustling is the coming into being of some land.

"To be a mouse," said *that poet.* To be a mouse. Vertiginous. Ripples. Afterward, they said it was poison. Half-a-Pole. Ha-alf... As if behind the whispering of clothes was a cut. From the slaughterhouse. And hidden in the rustling – blood. Even if it was only man-clothing. Alone, alone, – with the liquids of torture.

But rebbe, made of all things – of *this* and of *that* – you were so much one, – dirt, a torn book, and blood, – oh almost Transparency, – winter dance in the street, tattered jacket, man-snowdrifts (for everywhere was the sweat of poverty, – even in straw: there – in the wind, and the scattered handful of flour).

Life, rebbe.

And then, – here. This face... – all-embracing. It is as if you are walking through the city, and everywhere it is "mine," every corner of it. Vertiginous. Then – the ripples. And even if it was only: a garden (all this is the face, in the face) splashed out there – inaccesssibly. It sprang back, pain – as from glass. And – *you can-not squeeze in.* "A garden – just a garden." Like a popular tune. Bottomless. And – close at hand.

And how does it happen in the voice – some bottom lies concealed. And do we converse in words? Wind. Bottomless. You cannot name it – even with signs.

And this man from Hungary. Simply – a fraternal grave, no more. They dug him out – *with all the others* (and this is what matters most) into the light of Day, and suddenly – there was the Motherland. The question solved. *With all the others* (this matters most).

"God" – not the right expression. There is only: "And God?" For ever and ever.

And then – those journeys. Rol-ling stone. For prizes. And speeches. All correct. In honor of. And all – seems: floating-in-air! And as if through heaven it wan-ders: pain-language, – alone, – for heaven. All empty. Give up the ghost, – huddle up, – only pain. Language? – the Wind of the Universe.

Oh how simple it is. This "simple," there is no place for it in language. (You can try. Straight out will come – a thing. "The simple," – such Freedom – compare it: the mind brought collapse.)

Ripples. Simple, vertiginous.

Oh, whisperings, my clothing. Straw. T-r-a-sh. Oh, rustling, my skin. I-motherland, I such-clothing-and-flesh. With whispering-skin.

Ripples.

But no one cries out. That-is. Not I then. "I" is sticky. There is something other (behind – the whispering. Behind this rustling).

And in the water walks the sight of this Frenchman. Car-r-ion. What is this, – the essence? – the clothing? The one-ness.

Forget. Oh, when then. Forget. And – p u r i t y b e g i n s. And.

Ripples. With all the dirt – of torture.
No floating back up.
No-*Baptême*.
No-o.

1991

The Last Ravine

(PAUL CELAN)
To M. Broda

I go up;
thus in walking
one builds
a temple,
Breath of fraternity, – we are in this cloud:
I (with a word unknown to me
as if not in my mind) and wormwood (unquietly bitter
alongside me thrusting
this word upon me),
oh, once more
wormwood.
Clay,
sister.
And, of meanings, the one that was needless and central,
here (in these clods of the murdered)
seems a name to no purpose. With it
I am stained, going up
in simple – like fire – illumination,
to be marked with a final mark
in place – of a summit; like
an empty (since all is already abandoned)
face: like a place of painlessness
it rises – above the wormwood
(...
And

the form
was
not
seen
...)
But the cloud:
they grew blinder (in hollow facelessness),
the depths – without movement; the light
as from openedness – of stone.
Ever higher
and higher.

1983

Notes

With the exception of "A Snowdrop in the Storm," the Russian originals of all the prose texts given here are included in the large illustrated volume of Aygi's writings, *Razgovor na rasstoyanii* (Conversation at a Distance), published in St. Petersburg by Limbus Press in 2001. (The same volume also reprints the originals of the following poems: "Requiem before Winter"; "Kazimir Malevich"; "Degree: Of Stability"; "Reading Norwid"; and "Field: In the Full Blaze of Winter.") First publications of individual items are noted below.

Unless otherwise indicated, all English translations are published here for the first time.

A SNOWDROP IN THE STORM

First published in a booklet issued in Cheboksary, Chuvashia, in 1989 for the ninetieth anniversary of Sespel's birth. This translation first published in the online journal *Seedings* (No. 3).

Mikhail Sespel (in Chuvash, Sespel Mishi, 1899–1922) is one of the most powerful innovators in Chuvash poetry. Several of his poems in English translation are included in *An Anthology of Chuvash Poetry*, ed. Gennady Aygi, tr. Peter France (UNESCO Library of World Poetry, London, 1991). As part of its continued commitment to international poetry and works in translation, duration press has made available a digital version of the anthology on its website www.durationpress.com.

Translation made from Aygi's Russian version and included in *An Anthology of Chuvash Poetry* , ed. Gennady Aygi, tr. Peter France (UNESCO Library of World Poetry, London, 1991). As part of its continued commitment to international poetry and works in translation, duration press has made available a digital version of the anthology on its website www.durationpress.com.

EVERYDAY MIRACLE

First published in an abridged Swedish translation in *Artes* (the journal of the Swedish Academy) in 1990. First Russian publication in the journal *Druzhba narodov* (1993, No. 12).

Page 19: The writer and editor Olga Ivinskaya was Pasternak's friend and lover during the last thirteen years of his life.

Pavel Nikolaevich Vasiliev (1910–37) was a poet from Siberia who was executed in the purges; his writings include epic poems about the Siberian Cossacks.

Page 20: For an idea of the poems of the Chuvash poet Vasley Mitta (1908–57) see *An Anthology of Chuvash Poetry*.

Page 31: To "throw [the classics] overboard from the steamship of modernity" is a phrase from one the first futurist manifestos in Russia.

Page 36: Pimen is the monk/chronicler in Pushkin's *Boris Godunov*.

REQUIEM BEFORE WINTER

First Russian publication in Gennadij Ajgi, *Stichi 1954-1971*, ed. Wolfgang Kasack (Sagner, Munich, 1975) (henceforward "Kasack").

LEAVES – INTO A FESTIVE WIND

First published in Serbo-Croat translation in the journal *Kn'izhevna rech* (1985). First Russian publication in the journal *Druzhba narodov* (1994, No. 8).

Velimir (Viktor) Vladimirovich Khlebnikov (1885–1922) was the outstanding poet and theoretician of Russian Futurism. His collected works in English, translated by Paul Schmidt, are published by Harvard University Press.

Page 43: "Pook" is Kruchonykh's deliberately childish deformation of "book."

YES, KRUCHONYKH HIMSELF, OR THE LEAST
KNOWN OF THE MOST FAMOUS

First Russian publication in the journal *V mire knig* (1989, No. 4).

Alexsey Eliseevich Kruchonykh (1886–1968) was a Futurist poet and theorist, born into a peasant family in Kherson province. He was one of the principal champions of the transrational language use known as *zaum* (literally, "beyond mind"). His many word coinages include a series based on the word *zud* (itch); the collection *Zudutnye zudesa* appeared in 1922.

Page 56: "Forgot to hang myself" is the first line of a short Kruchonykh poem of 1913.

KRCH – 80

First Russian publication in Gennady Aygi, *Otmechennaya zima*, ed. Véronique Lossky (Sintaksis, Paris, 1982). This translation first published in Gennady Aygi, *Winter Revels and Ever Further into the Snows,* tr. Peter France (Rumor Books, San Francisco, 2009). See also a translation by Edwin Morgan in his *Collected Translations* (Carcanet Press, Manchester, 1996).

MAYAKOVSKY
First Russian publication in *Literaturnaya gazeta* (July 14, 1993).

IN HONOR OF A MASTER
First Russian publication as an introduction to a book of poems by Kazimir Malevich, *Po lestnitse poznaniya* (On the Stairway of Knowledge) (Gileya, Moscow, 1991).

KAZIMIR MALEVICH
First Russian publication in Kasack. This translation first published in *Comparative Criticism* 4 (1982), reprinted in Gennady Aygi, *Selected Poems 1954–1994*, tr. Peter France (Angel Books, London, and Hydra Books, Evanston, IL, 1997).

Page 68: The boards referred to here are the wooden base for icon painting.

Vitebsk, Chagall's native town, was the site of the UNOVIS art school where Malevich and Lissitzky (El) worked.

"Velimir" is Khlebnikov.

Daniil Kharms was a leading avant-garde poet of the 1920s.

Before his death, Malevich made a suprematist sketch for his own coffin.

MASSACRE OF A SILK FLAG
First published (in Danish and Russian) in *Vladimir Jakovlev. Tekster af Gennadij Aigi og Jindrich Chalupesky* (Borgen, Copenhagen, 1976).

The remarkable painter Vladimir Igorevich Yakovlev was born in 1934 (the same year as Aygi), and died in 1998 after many years of severe mental illness and near-blindness. One of his portraits of Aygi is used as the frontispiece for the present volume.

TWO POEMS FOR VLADIMIR YAKOVLEV

"Windows on Trubnaya Square in Spring": first Russian publication in Kasack; Yakovlev made a painting inspired by this poem.

"Good Mornings": first Russian publication in *Aygi, Otmechennaya zima*. This translation first published in Aygi, *Winter Revels and Ever Further into the Snows*.

Page 73: The Patriarchal Ponds are a well-known landmark in Moscow.

AN EVENING WITH SHALAMOV

First Russian publication in the journal *Vestnik RKhD* (Paris, 1982, No. 137).

Varlam Tikhonovich Shalamov (1907–82) was a prose writer and poet, chiefly known for his *Kolyma Tales*, dispassionate depictions of life in the Soviet forced labor camps where he spent many years for unknown "crimes."

Page 75: Aygi's friend Konstantin Bogatyryov was a poet and translator of Rilke; he was murdered in 1976.

DEGREE: OF STABILITY

First Russian publication in Kasack. This translation first published in Gennady Aygi, *Degree: Of Stability,* tr. Peter France (Duration Press, Sausalito, CA, 1999).

O YES: LIGHT OF KAFKA

Text written for a special number of the Danish journal *Cras* (1984, No. 39), devoted to Kafka's centenary and containing poems by Aygi and etchings by Igor Makarevich. First Russian publication in the volume of 2001. First English publication in the anthology *Two Lines: Some Kind of Beautiful Signal* (Two Lines Press, San Francisco, 2010).

First Russian publication in Kasack. This translation first published in Aygi, *Selected Poems*.

READING NORWID

First Russian publication, in a different (shorter) version, in *Otmechennaya zima*. Also a somewhat longer version in Gennady Aygi, *Teper' vsegda snega* (Sovetsky Pisatel, Moscow, 1992).

Cyprian Kamil Norwid (1821–83) was one of the leading Polish poets of the nineteenth century (for an idea of his poetry see *Selected Poems*, tr. Adam Czerniawski [Anvil Press, London, 2004]). He was particularly important to Aygi in the late 1970s.

The dedicatee is Wiktor Woroszylski (1927–96), Polish poet, writer, and scholar of Russian literature, author of *The Life of Mayakovsky*, and a close friend of Aygi.

Page 95: "Janowska Street" was the site of a Nazi forced labor camp for Polish Jews.

On the expression "super-Place" see "O Yes: the Smile of Max Jacob."

Page 96: "Powązki" is the principal cemetery in Warsaw, with many graves of participants in the Warsaw Uprising.

"Frycek" was Chopin's childhood name.

BAUDELAIRE

Written originally in Chuvash. First Russian publication in Kasack.

O YES: THE SMILE OF MAX JACOB

First Russian publication in the journal *Literaturnoe Obozrenie* (1998, Nos. 5 and 6).

Originally written as the preface to an (unpublished) cycle of poems connected with the French poet Max Jacob (1876–1944).

Page 103: Saint-Benoît: the abbey of Saint-Benoît-sur-Loire where Jacob lived for the last years of his life, before being arrested by the Gestapo as a Jew.

RENÉ CHAR

Telephone interview conducted by Igor Pomerantsev for the BBC Russian service of the BBC. Published in French translation in Guennadi Aïgui, *Conversations à distance*, tr. Léon Robel (Éditions Circé, Saulxures, 1994). First Russian publication in Aygi, *Razgovor na rasstoyanii* . This translation first published in the online journal *Seedings* (No. 3).

The poet René Char (1907–88) was born in L'Isle-sur-la-Sorgue in the south of France and lived there off and on for most of his life.

FIELD: IN THE FULL BLAZE OF WINTER

First Russian publication in Kasack. This translation first published in Aygi, *Selected Poems*. See also translation by Edwin Morgan in his *Collected Translations*.

ON THE POETRY OF TOMAS TRANSTRÖMER

First Russian publication (partial) in the newspaper *Segodnya* (May 7, 1994) and the journal *Inostrannaya literatura* (1995, No. 9) as introductions to selections of poems by the Swedish poet Tomas Tranströmer (1931–2015), who won the Nobel Prize in Literature in 2011. See Tomas Tranströmer, *The Great Enigma: New Collected Poems* (New Directions, New York 2006).

First published in Léon Robel's French translation in the review *Le Nouveau Commerce* 81 (Autumn 1991). First Russian publication in Gennady Aygi, *Prodolzhenie ot'ezda* (Proekt OGI Moscow, 2001). This translation first published in Gennady Aygi, *Field-Russia*, tr. Peter France (New Directions, New York, 2007).

There are many references to the German poet Paul Celan (1920–70) in Aygi's work of the 1980s, particularly in the collection "Time of Ravines" (in Aygi, *Field-Russia*). This poetic tribute alludes to Celan's suicide by drowning in the Seine in Paris.

Page 112: "That poet" is the Polish poet Aleksander Wat (1900–1967).

Page 113: "This man from Hungary" is the Hungarian poet Miklós Radnóti (1909–44).

First Russian publication in Guennadi Aïgui, *Le Temps des ravins*, bilingual edition, tr. Léon Robel (Nouveau Commerce, Paris, 1990). This translation first published in Aygi, *Field-Russia*.

New Directions Paperbooks — a partial listing

Martín Adán, The Cardboard House
César Aira, Ema, the Captive
  An Episode in the Life of a Landscape Painter
  Ghosts
Will Alexander, The Sri Lankan Loxodrome
Paul Auster, The Red Notebook
Honoré de Balzac, Colonel Chabert
Djuna Barnes, Nightwood
Charles Baudelaire, The Flowers of Evil*
Bei Dao, City Gate, Open Up
Nina Berberova, The Ladies From St. Petersburg
Max Blecher, Adventures in Immediate Irreality
Roberto Bolaño, By Night in Chile
  Distant Star
  Last Evenings on Earth
  Nazi Literature in the Americas
Jorge Luis Borges, Labyrinths
  Professor Borges
  Seven Nights
Coral Bracho, Firefly Under the Tongue*
Kamau Brathwaite, Ancestors
Basil Bunting, Complete Poems
Anne Carson, Antigonick
  Glass, Irony & God
Horacio Castellanos Moya, Senselessness
Louis-Ferdinand Céline
  Death on the Installment Plan
  Journey to the End of the Night
Rafael Chirbes, On the Edge
Inger Christensen, alphabet
Jean Cocteau, The Holy Terrors
Peter Cole, The Invention of Influence
Julio Cortázar, Cronopios & Famas
Albert Cossery, The Colors of Infamy
Robert Creeley, If I Were Writing This
Guy Davenport, 7 Greeks
Osamu Dazai, No Longer Human
H.D., Tribute to Freud
  Trilogy
Helen DeWitt, The Last Samurai
Robert Duncan, Selected Poems
Eça de Queirós, The Maias
William Empson, 7 Types of Ambiguity
Shusaku Endo, Deep River
Jenny Erpenbeck, The End of Days
  Visitation
Lawrence Ferlinghetti
  A Coney Island of the Mind

F. Scott Fitzgerald, The Crack-Up
  On Booze
Forrest Gander, The Trace
Henry Green, Pack My Bag
Allen Grossman, Descartes' Loneliness
John Hawkes, Travesty
Felisberto Hernández, Piano Stories
Hermann Hesse, Siddhartha
Takashi Hiraide, The Guest Cat
Yoel Hoffman, Moods
Susan Howe, My Emily Dickinson
  That This
Bohumil Hrabal, I Served the King of England
Sonallah Ibrahim, That Smell
Christopher Isherwood, The Berlin Stories
Fleur Jaeggy, Sweet Days of Discipline
Alfred Jarry, Ubu Roi
B.S. Johnson, House Mother Normal
James Joyce, Stephen Hero
Franz Kafka, Amerika: The Man Who Disappeared
John Keene, Counternarratives
Laszlo Krasznahorkai, Satantango
  The Melancholy of Resistance
  Seiobo There Below
Eka Kurniawan, Beauty Is a Wound
Rachel Kushner, The Strange Case of Rachel K
Mme. de Lafayette, The Princess of Clèves
Lautréamont, Maldoror
Sylvia Legris, The Hideous Hidden
Denise Levertov, Selected Poems
Li Po, Selected Poems
Clarice Lispector, The Hour of the Star
  Near to the Wild Heart
  The Passion According to G. H.
Federico García Lorca, Selected Poems*
  Three Tragedies
Nathaniel Mackey, Splay Anthem
Stéphane Mallarmé, Selected Poetry and Prose*
Norman Manea, Captives
Javier Marías, Your Face Tomorrow (3 volumes)
Bernadette Mayer, Works & Days
Thomas Merton, New Seeds of Contemplation
  The Way of Chuang Tzu
Henri Michaux, Selected Writings
Dunya Mikhail, The War Works Hard
Henry Miller, The Colossus of Maroussi
  Big Sur & The Oranges of Hieronymus Bosch

*BILINGUAL EDITIO
For a complete listing,
or visit us online at nd

e, New York, NY 10011